Revise Mark's Gospel for GCSE

Simon and Christopher Danes

Second edition

ST MARK'S PRESS

Photocopying this book

Small runs of a few pages are permissible. However, if you wish to make a large number of copies, or to copy more than ten pages or so, please contact the publisher on email or phone. Permission will normally be granted, in exchange for a small fee. Forgive us, but authors depend on their royalties for their livelihoods, and to make copies without paying a fee is to deprive authors of their incomes.

Also available for GCSE revision:

Mark's Gospel on double CD

St Mark's Press, £12.99
Available from www.stmarkspress.com
ISBN 978-1-907062-01-8

This double CD of Mark's Gospel is an excellent revision aid and many students have found it very useful indeed. Listening to the text is a very effective way of revising it. Actor Peter Wickham has recorded over 200 talking books; he acts, rather than reads the story, which makes it easier to learn. The Guardian's review called this 'Peter Wickham's brilliant reading' and £1 for each copy sold goes to Christian Aid, a charity which helps people in the developing world.

Contents

How to revise

This advice is based on the experiences of students who've revised successfully for their GCSEs. We hope it's helpful. And good luck!

General advice

Religious Studies is one of those subjects that takes a lot of revision. Not all GCSEs do. With some, you build up your skills over the course, then the exam tests them. This is to some extent the case with, say, English Language and modern languages: you can brush up your knowledge for them, but you can't really cram your head with knowledge.

RS is rather different, because the exam does test a lot of knowledge – and other skills as well. So, you're going to need to allocate a lot of time to it.

I used to say to students that they should give at least 20 hours to RS revision. That sounds a lot. It is, but then it isn't a lot if you do one hour a day for 20 days. The best way to get high marks is simply to learn the material. For example, if you're studying Mark's Gospel, up to about 40% of the marks can just be on how well you know the stories or accounts in Mark. That's not difficult but it does take time to learn them.

Anyone who wanted to make a fortune should invent a machine for GCSE candidates which would revise for them. Unfortunately, there's no such thing. If you want to do well, it's up to you.

One of the most painless ways to revise is to review your work throughout the course. If you look back on your notes and set texts during the holidays, for example, it will help to keep it fresh in your memory. Frequently reviewing your work helps you to learn it for the final exam.

There are some people who manage this, but in general, most of us don't! So we have to learn it much later. Still, the sooner you start, the better. Even ten minutes a day makes a difference, once you're in your exam year.

So, here are some dos and don'ts for revising. You can apply lots of them to your other subjects; they work for other things as well as GCSE RS.

Don'ts

1. **Don't panic!**

2. **Don't try silly methods of revising.** Dictating all your notes onto an audio recording will take ages. By the time you've finished, the exam will be over. And when will you have time to listen to them all? Writing out all your notes again is a waste of time. You might well find that you're doing this mechanically, without concentrating. There's no point in it, anyway, because you've already got a copy of your notes! If you're still considering this method, think for a moment. How long does it take you to write a page? How long, then, will it take to write ten pages? How long to write out all your notes again?!

3. **Don't waste time.** It's very easy to do three minutes' work in an hour. You might spend the first five minutes arranging your pens and pencils on the desk, then look out of the window, then make a cup of coffee, then decide to send a few texts... Before you know it, the time you had earmarked for revision will have gone! Be strict with yourself. Stick to your revision timetable.

4. **Don't simply not bother working or rely on cramming it all in on one night before the exam. It won't work.**

5. **Don't work in an atmosphere in which you can't concentrate properly.** Get away from the radio, TV, computer games, mobile phone, dog, noisy younger brothers and sisters...! If you can't find somewhere to work in peace at home, try staying on after school (maybe in the library) or going in before school starts. Or try the local public library.

6. **Don't try to do anything else which needs your concentration when you're revising.** Music's a good thing. Some people claim it helps. Others say it distracts you and this is probably right (though

everyone's different). You need your full attention on your work if you're going to learn effectively. You can't revise and watch TV at the same time, either.

7. Don't revise in bed. You will fall asleep.

8. Don't stay in bed all day when you're not in school. Getting up early gives you more time for work!

Dos

1. Do plan your day and make a revision timetable. If you're on study leave, try to do three (or even four) hours' work before lunchtime. This will break the back of it. If you're on study leave, try to do a full day's work (7 hours? It sounds a lot but it can be done).

When you **plan your revision timetable:**

1. You'll have a lot of work to do while you're still in school, including homework. But keep the revision ticking over. Two small chunks a day of ten minutes each make a huge difference in the long run – if you start now.
2. Break each day, when you're on study leave, into three blocks: morning, afternoon and evening. Work for two out of three of these. If you want to go out or to relax, plan it in. Don't let friends who don't want to revise try to lure you away! It makes them feel better, but it doesn't help you.
3. Break up each day into different subjects. Then break those subjects into topics. So, you could do:

   9 - 10 a.m.:   Mark's Gospel: learn some texts

   10-11a.m.:   Geography: settlements.

   11-11.20 a.m.:   Break.

   11.20 a.m. to 12 noon: English Literature: read Act One of *Macbeth*.

4. The revision timetable is a framework, not a straightjacket. Keep fairly strictly to it for the first couple of days. Pencil in the rest of the week.

5. Little and often helps. Don't set one block aside for each subject; you'll need to go back to it to brush up on it. At the end of each day, going over your notes for the last time is a good idea, too.

6. You'll find when you go over stuff again that you won't remember some of what you thought you'd learnt. This is maddening but try not to let it annoy you too much. It's inevitable. The vast majority will have stuck. Some bits just don't seem to want to go in. It can be worth making a note of them and reviewing them often, until they've stuck.

7. The most common problem with students doing revision is that they simply don't do enough work. However, for a minority of people, there can be the reverse problem of doing too much. Some students are over conscientious and panic if they're not working every second of every day. If this applies to you, do slow down. You need to do enough work – *and no more.* If you're working seven or eight hour days, that's plenty. Working twelve, fifteen or eighteen hours a day isn't necessary and is counter productive: you'll get stressed and tired, and this is likely to decrease the effectiveness of your revision. Exercise and relaxing are actually important parts of the revision process. You need to give your brain time to relax; it makes it more effective in the long run.

2. **Do use anything you find helpful:**
- Try **active reading**, rather than just reading. In Mark's Gospel, for example, highlight the word 'Pharisees' in blue, 'Peter' in red, 'scribes' in yellow... Scribble some notes, even if you throw them away. Turn the book over after every page and say aloud what you can remember of it. Draw a sketch of what happened (can you get the whole story into one picture?).
- Use:
  → **spider diagrams**
  → **cue cards** in colour – easier to remember than if they're in black and white. Some people learn best in a visual way. But all of us can use this technique; it isn't the case that we only learn in one way and not in another. You may well find, after a while, that you actually picture the cue card or spider diagram in your

head when you recall the information, and that you remember where on the page and what colour the bit of information is. (And if you don't, it doesn't matter: the important thing is that the stuff has gone in.)

→ **mind maps**
→ make **reduced notes**... write down the key points. Try and boil down the information into the most compact form possible. It helps to do this fairly neatly, too: messy scribbles are depressing to revise from and again, the very act of writing something down helps you to learn it.
→ And do use **pictures**: they stick in the mind.
→ **Read**: if you're going to revise by reading your notes through (it works for some people), how many times do you need to do so before they stick? If it's five times, better to do it once a day for five days, than five times in one sitting. Active reading, though, tends to be better than simply reading – but again, you have to find what works best for you.
→ Use **spot learning** techniques. For things that need to be learnt 100%, like quotations, foreign language vocab, formulae, dates and so on, it's worth making a card and sticking it up somewhere in the house (the bathroom or the front of the fridge is a good place!). Every time you go past it, stop, and read it. It will probably take ten seconds at the most to do so. In a couple of weeks, you'll have read it several hundred times. It'll stick, and it's painless. It's a good idea to get your spot learning cards up as soon as possible.

More on revising GCSE RS

Your teachers can help. Find out which specification (syllabus) you're studying for. Find the exam board's website and look at the content of the specification. This book gives notes on all of Mark's Gospel, but none of the boards sets the entire Gospel. (Different boards set slightly different sections. We've included all of Mark so that the book can be used for all the boards.) Find out which sections you need to know and ignore the rest. There's no point in revising things you don't need to know for the exam.

After the notes on the text of Mark, there's a section called 'Revision notes on Mark and Christianity today'. This covers:
1. The authority of Mark's Gospel for Christians today
2. The Trinity and beliefs about Jesus
3. Baptism
4. The Eucharist / the Mass
5. Persecution and Christianity today
6. Mark and community cohesion.

Again, not all of the boards set all of these topics, so you need to find out which ones are set by your board and then don't worry about the others.

You can also look at past papers – and, even more importantly, how they're marked – on the website. And make sure you understand what the examiner's looking for. Try writing some model answers and then mark them, using the website's mark scheme.

Up to around 40% of the final marks can test how well you know the set texts of Mark's Gospel – the bits you need to learn for the exam. You can easily gain high marks here by learning all the set texts **in detail.** You can't read the Gospel too many times. Get a copy of it and keep it in your jacket pocket, and read it when you're waiting for a bus or you're in the lunch queue. Keep going over and over it. Highlight the bits you don't yet know (there are some little details it's easy to forget) and then make a note of them on a postcard – and look at the postcard when you've got a spare moment.

This is an advert, but do buy and use the CD of Mark's Gospel from St Mark's Press! (You can order it on our website, www.stmarkspress.com .) It's a very dramatic recording. That makes it easier to learn the texts, because you'll remember how Peter Wickham reads it. Listen to it for five or ten minutes a day. Stop the CD in the middle of a story and say aloud what happens next.

For a learning tool and to test your knowledge, use the questions – 'How well do you know Mark's Gospel?' – at the back of this book. If you can, get someone to ask you the questions. Make a note of the ones you don't know. Keep going back to the questions; you'll find your score increases the more you do it.

Also, make sure you know what the stories mean. You can be asked questions on this. The notes you have made in the course and in this book will help.

For all the GCSE RS papers, you're going to be asked your own opinions about things. Look carefully at the wording. It usually says something like 'Give reasons for your answer, showing that you have thought about more than one point of view.' It sometimes adds: 'You must refer to Christianity [or 'Mark's Gospel'] in your answer.'

You've got to do *exactly* what these questions tell you if you want full marks.

They're usually marked out of five. **This doesn't mean you have to make five points.** Note:

- If you just give your own view, however good what you say is, you can't get more than 3 marks. You'll have thrown two marks away.
- If it specifies that you must refer to Christianity or to Mark's Gospel, make sure you do. Otherwise, you can't get more than 3 out of 5 marks. (This happens a lot on any papers about modern ethical / moral issues. It's perfectly possible to talk about war, say, without once mentioning Christianity. However, the examiners justify knocking marks off like this by saying it's an RS exam, so it's got to have something about religion in it. So, make sure you bring in specifically *Christian* views.)

To write the best answers you these sort of questions, you need to do this:

1. Say what you think.
2. Explain why and give some evidence. Referring to a specific section from Mark is a good way forward (e.g. 'Christians should give money to the poor because Jesus told the rich man in the story to sell everything he had and give to the poor, and that he would then have treasure in heaven').
3. Say why someone might disagree with you. ('However, others would disagree because they would say...' and give some detail on why they disagree.)
4. Say why you disagree with them! (Who's got the stronger argument, and why?)
5. Perhaps end with a single sentence that re-states your view: 'So, I think that... because this seems to me the strongest argument.'

If you do this well, you should get 5/5 marks - and you want to get as many marks as you can!

While this is a book about Mark's Gospel, you may well be studying modern ethics / morality and Christianity. If so, it's worth considering these points:

- Make sure you know what the religion you're studying teaches about these issues. Be as specific as you can. Sometimes, everyone in the faith will think the same thing. (All Christians think murder is wrong!) However, there'll be disagreement on things like abortion or contraception. Where there are differences, show the examiner you know about them.
- If you're studying Christianity and morality, linking things back to the teaching of Jesus or the Bible is always good. If you're doing Mark as well, you have an advantage, because you can bring in what Mark says. For example, 'Jesus was against racism. He healed the daughter of the Syro-Phoenician woman, even though she was of a different race.'
- Some students find reading up on the issues from a different book is helpful. We publish *Today's Issues and Christian Beliefs,* which is a very popular GCSE textbook and you can get it through our website. (Yes, OK: sorry about the advert.)

Sitting the exam

- **Don't panic!** Nobody likes exams. You'll be fine, if you've revised properly.
- **Do use your time properly.** Take a watch in with you. Make sure you finish the paper. Practise how long it takes you to answer the different types of questions. If you just need to write a sentence (or a few words), don't write a paragraph – it wastes precious time and it can't get you any more marks. If you need to write a paragraph or two, don't just write a sentence or you'll lose marks.
- **Do read the paper thoroughly before you start** and make sure you know which questions you have to answer.
- **Never leave gaps,** even if you don't know the answer. **The maximum mark you can get for a gap is 0. Examiners comment that more marks are lost in the exam through students leaving gaps, than through their not revising**

thoroughly. If you don't know the answer, make an intelligent guess. This may be totally right, in which case you'll get full marks. Or it may just pick up a couple of marks – but they're still worth having.

- **Do check the number of marks available for each question.** A five mark question is going to need a longer answer than a one mark question. Some people think five marks means you've got to make five points. **They're wrong.** In GCSE RS, marks are awarded by the quality of the answer. So, an excellent answer will get five marks, an OK answer will get 3 marks, and a bad answer may get one mark. Detail's usually good, but don't bother with lots of detail for a one mark question.

- Do write as clearly as you can, and in good English. The examiners have to award marks for good English. If they can't read what you've written (they'll try, but they can't work miracles), you'll lose marks. It sounds daft to say it but you should offer your best work in exams.

- **Do answer the question.** Candidates do misread questions. A good answer to a non-existent question gets zero marks. Something that's even more common is not answering every *part* of the question. This again loses marks.

- **Saying the same thing in three different ways is not the same as using three examples.** Some people get a bee in their bonnet and then use the same example for every question. Don't. Use different examples where you can.

- **Don't waffle. Make sure your answer is relevant.** The exam tests your knowledge of the course by *sampling* that knowledge. Not everything will come up. Don't try to say, 'Ms Examiner, I know lots about this course so I'm going to write down something you haven't asked for!'

- **Try to allow yourself time to check your answers.** Don't worry if you haven't done this. Some people rush through exams and then have a little sleep because they're tired! This may be because they're geniuses. Or it could be because they're very silly. (Which do you think is more likely?) But if you do have time, check:
  - Are your answers correct?
  - When you need to give detail, have you given as much detail as

you can, or have you left something out?

- Have you answered the question set? Check with the question paper.
- Be careful not to panic when you check your answers. Believe that you're good at the subject! Some people can think that one of their answers is bound to be wrong, so they cross out the right answer and put the wrong one in.

Finally, good luck! We hope you find this book helpful; do email us through our website with your comments.

When we give suggestions for how to revise
during the revision notes themselves,

they're in smaller type and in italics

and are introduced by the words

Revision tip

Revision notes on Mark's Gospel

You won't need to use all of these notes. Check which passages and topics you need to revise for the specification you're studying and ignore the rest.

It's worth using 'active reading' techniques: see p.4.

Why were the Gospels written?

Mark is one of the four Gospels. 'Gospel' translates the Greek word which means 'good news'.

Four main reasons for writing the Gospels were:

1. Jesus' disciples, the original witnesses, were dying off. A permanent record was needed.

2. Gentiles (non-Jews) came into the community of the Church. They came in great numbers, from different religious backgrounds. There was a danger they might bring wrong ideas into Christianity. The Gospel writers wanted to put the record straight about Jesus.

3. The Roman authorities needed to be shown that Christianity was not politically dangerous.

4. Christians needed to be encouraged in their faith.

Who was Mark?

He may well have been the 'John Mark' who appears in The Acts of the Apostles and in the letters of Paul and Peter in the New Testament. John Mark's home was in Jerusalem and he was a travelling companion of Paul.

Christian tradition also links Mark with Peter, the leader of the disciples. Papias, writing 100 years after Jesus' crucifixion, makes this claim. He said this information came from a still earlier writer, who said that Mark was Peter's helper, and that he wrote down the stories Peter told when he was preaching.

We need to be slightly careful here. 'Mark' was a very common name in the Roman Empire. But if Mark was not John Mark, we know nothing about him.

When and where was the Gospel written?

The answer is, probably in AD 64-65 in Rome.

This would fit in with the fact that the Emperor Nero was killing Christians in Rome in AD 64. Paul and Peter died in this persecution. Mark emphasizes that his readers should stand firm in the face of trouble. This would fit with the Roman situation. He uses some Latin words instead of Greek ones. (The Gospel itself was written in Greek.)

Again, we cannot be certain. Some scholars believe there is not enough evidence. Others suggest the Gospel is even earlier. Few believe it to be later.

What were Mark's sources?

It is difficult to be certain about written sources, since we do not have them, if they ever existed. Mark would certainly have used stories about Jesus that circulated by word of mouth (orally). He may have consulted Peter.

Written sources may have been used for:

1. The Passion (the story of Jesus' suffering and death).
2. The Little Apocalypse (chapter 13, speaking of the end of the world).
3. And some stories may have been in Aramaic, the language spoken in Palestine at that time. Peter and Jesus would have spoken Aramaic. The Aramaic sources may have been spoken or written, or both.

Mark chapter 1

The preaching of John the Baptist
Read Mark 1.1-8

Mark opens his book by calling it the 'good news' or 'gospel'. The good news is about Jesus, who is the Messiah (Christ) and the Son of God.

John's coming fits in with the Old Testament: the prophets Isaiah and Malachi predicted that someone would arrive to prepare for the

Messiah. The Jews believed this would be Elijah. John lived in the desert like Elijah, and his clothes – the camel hair garment and the leather belt – are identical. Jesus later implies that John is the expected Elijah (Mark 9.13).

John calls on the people to repent. This is more than just to say they're sorry; it means to change their minds and their attitudes. He baptizes, or washes, them as a sign that they have done this. (Remember: this is not the same as Christian baptism, though Christian baptism grew out of it.)

The Messiah is so great, John says, that he is unworthy to undo the Messiah's sandal strap. This was a slave's duty for his master. The Messiah will baptize 'with the Holy Spirit'. This probably means he will bring people in touch with God in a new way. Mark's first readers might well be reminded here of their own baptisms.

Some scholars have suggested that John was once an Essene.

The **Essenes** lived a kind of monastic life. Some lived in towns; most lived in the Judean desert. They believed themselves to be the only true Jews, and they had strict rules. Many did not marry, or only did so to produce children. Training for the group was hard and long. They shared their property, and may have written the Dead Sea Scrolls, found at Qumran in 1948. Like John, they baptized their members, although unlike John, they baptized them more than once. They were also waiting for not one, but two (perhaps three) Messiahs.

Jesus' baptism and temptation
Read Mark 1.9-13

Jesus first appears in Mark at the baptism. Three things should be noticed:

1. The heavens open. Jewish writings which look forward to the Kingdom of God sometimes include the idea that God will open heaven (Isaiah 64.1, for example). The detail shows that the Kingdom is almost here.

2. The Holy Spirit descends like a dove. The Holy Spirit had inspired the Old Testament prophets. People thought he would return with the Messiah.

Saying that the Spirit descended 'like a dove' may remind Mark's readers of the dove which brought the olive branch to Noah when

the flood was over, or it may echo the story of creation in Genesis, when God's Spirit hovers (like a bird?) over the unmade world.
3. There is a voice from heaven. The voice of God uses words from Psalm 2.7, originally addressed to Israel's king, to say that Jesus is the Son of God.

The voice also says God is pleased with Jesus. This echoes Isaiah 42.1, which speaks about someone called the Servant of the Lord (or the Suffering Servant). It's not clear who the author of Isaiah meant him to be, but he was said to have died for the people. This is what Jesus will do.

Jesus, then, is called the **Son of God**. In the Old Testament, the king was called the son of God. The Messiah was the king (see below), so calling Jesus 'the Son of God' shows he is a kingly Messiah.

Jesus does not often call himself 'the Son of God', though he does not deny being the Son of God. He does not want people to get the wrong idea about the sort of Messiah he is. He is not the warrior king the Zealots hoped for: his path is one of suffering.

Christians soon came to realize that Jesus was God himself, made man. 'Son of God' became a good way of expressing this idea.

Mark does not go into details about Jesus' temptation by the Devil. 'Temptation' means 'being put to the test': since Jesus withstands the test of the Devil, he is ready to start his work. Mark may be telling his readers that they should not worry about being tempted to do wrong as long as they stand firm, perhaps in the face of persecution. After all, Jesus was tempted too.

The Jews believed the Kingdom of God (see pp. 24ff for more details) would involve a struggle against the forces of evil. Jesus begins this battle against the Devil here, and it continues when he casts out demons.

Jesus calls the first disciples
Read Mark 1.14-20

Jesus' words in verse 15 give Mark's summary of the whole of Jesus' message. It is deliberately placed at the beginning of Jesus' work:

> The time has come;
> the Kingdom of God is at hand.
> Repent
> and believe the good news.

(Mark 1.14)

Revision tip:

It is worth learning this verse. The layout of the quotation may make this easier: learn one line at a time. Suggestion: use spot learning techniques for this.)

- 'Disciples' means 'people who learn'.
- Other Jewish teachers had disciples. Jesus is unique in that he 'calls' his disciples. He does not wait for them to come to him; he seeks them out.
- Jesus' disciples are ordinary people, not just educated men: his message is for all.
- The four fishermen – Simon (Peter), Andrew, James and John – follow Jesus 'immediately'. This is how Mark thinks people should respond to Jesus' call.
- They will no longer catch fish: their catch will be people. They will get others to follow Jesus, to draw them into the 'net' of the Kingdom.

The first miracle in Mark
Read Mark 1.21-28

This takes place in the synagogue in Capernaum, where Jesus taught. He probably preached the sermon, as any adult male could do. His teaching was 'new' and 'with authority', unlike that of the teachers of the Law or scribes.

The **scribes** spent their time studying the Torah and trying to apply it to everyday life. Many of them were also Pharisees, though some were Sadducees.

Jews in Jesus' time believed in demons, and thought that they caused illness. Some have suggested the man in Mark's story here was mentally ill. This may be true, but it is not the point Mark is trying to make. Jesus defeats the demon by exorcizing it. This defeat of the evil powers shows that the Kingdom has arrived.

The demon recognizes Jesus, but he orders it to be silent. The theme of Jesus no allowing news of his identity to be spread is common in Mark. He also refuses to let people say who he is in public: they are not to go around saying he is the Messiah. This theme is called the **Messianic Secret**. Various ideas have been suggested as to why Jesus does this. A good explanation is that he did not want people to get too excited. If they went around saying he was the Messiah, they might think the final showdown with the Romans was about to start. Jesus needed to teach his disciples and others what being the Messiah meant. Only then could they call him 'Messiah'.

The healing of Simon Peter's mother-in-law
Read Mark 1.29-31

This story may originally have come from Simon Peter himself. Jesus does not perform his miracles for show; this one takes place in private. As with the other healings, it shows Jesus' compassion and care. When she is cured, Peter's mother-in-law begins to wait on Jesus and his disciples. Mark may be hinting that, just as she served Jesus at table, Christians should serve Jesus in their lives.

If Mark thinks the fever was caused by a demon, he does not say so.

The healing of many people
Read Mark 1.32-34

The summaries of healing miracles show the sort of thing Mark thought Jesus did. There are three of them: 1.32-34, 3.7-12 and 6.53-56.

Jesus heals a large number of people, showing that he has compassion and that the Kingdom is coming. Again, he refuses to let the demons identify him.

Jesus preaches in Galilee
Read Mark 1.35-39

Jesus and his disciples go on a preaching tour throughout Galilee.

Jesus prays early in the morning. He was a Jew and it was Jewish practice in his time, as it is now, to do this. But Mark may also want the people to understand what sort of a Messiah Jesus is: he needs strength to carry on his work, as he has just performed a large number of miracles.

Simon Peter and his 'companions' (probably the other disciples) find him. Everyone is looking for Jesus. Mark believed they still were, when he wrote, and Christians believe they still are today. People need Jesus, even if they do not realize it.

Jesus says they must go to the other villages, so that he can preach there, too, because 'that is why I came'. He has just come from Capernaum, but originally he came from God.

The preaching tour is dealt with in one verse but it would have taken many months. 'Driving out demons' and 'preaching' are both the work of the Messiah, who brings in the Kingdom.

Jesus heals a leper
Read Mark 1.40-45

The Torah is the Jewish Law, contained in the first five books of the Bible, which were believed to have been written by Moses. It said people with leprosy were outside God's chosen people: outcasts. They were ceremonially impure and they had to stay away from everyone else. People were so afraid of the disease that they classed many skin complaints as 'leprosy', to be on the safe side. Whether the man in the story had what we would now call leprosy, or something else, is unclear.

Jesus cures the man by touching him and by a word of command. His power to heal comes from his own authority: it is not magic. Touching a leper would have been very shocking: he risked catching the disease and would also have become ceremonially impure, according to the Torah.

Jesus is moved by 'pity' (some early Greek copies of Mark say he is moved by 'anger': anger that the leper had suffered so much). He tells the man to go and make the sacrifice laid down by the Torah, and to show himself to the priest. The priest would check that he was cured. This allowed him back into society – a miracle with follow-up care as well!

The account ends with a repeat of the Messianic Secret theme. Despite Jesus' command to the man to be quiet, the news spreads fast. People with leprosy were outcasts from Judaism, but they are acceptable to Jesus. The Kingdom is open to them, too.

Revision tip:

Go back and read the whole of Mark chapter 1 again, or listen to it on CD –
or at least the sections you need to know for the exam.
After a few hours, go back and read it once more!

Mark chapter 2

Jesus heals a paralysed man
Read Mark 2.1-12

A very vivid story. The flat roofs in Israel were made from mud plastered over branches, so it would be easy to dig through them.

People thought sin sometimes caused illness, so Jesus says the man's sins are forgiven. Perhaps the man thought he was ill because he was being punished by God. If so, Jesus' words would have been a great reassurance. The arrival of the Kingdom brings forgiveness.

Yet only God could forgive sins. That was why Jesus' words appeared blasphemous to the scribes. (It is not clear whether these scribes or teachers of the Law were Pharisees or Sadducees.) Jesus tries to show them that what he says is true. Saying 'Your sins are forgiven' is no harder than saying, 'Get up, pick up your bed and walk.' He shows this is true by telling the man to take up his mat and go home – and the man does just that.

Note:
- Although the paralysed man's faith is not mentioned, the faith of his friends is important. This faith forms a kind of friendship with Jesus. All the miracles in Mark come about because faith already exists. The scribes do not have this faith in Jesus.

- Jesus does something only God can do: he forgives sins. Mark thus hints at who Jesus really is.
- Jesus is in conflict with the authorities. Already, there is a hint of the opposition that will lead to Jesus' death.

The Pharisees meet with the Herodians ('Herod's party' in the Good News Bible) to discuss how to destroy Jesus. Again, we have a reference early on in the Gospel to his death. We know practically nothing about the Herodians. Presumably, they were the supporters of Herod Antipas, the ruler of Galilee. The Pharisees thought very little of Herod. If they were willing to meet with his followers, they were getting very anxious.

Jesus calls Levi
Read Mark 2.13-17

Levi may also have been called Matthew. He was a tax collector.

Tax collectors were hated because they worked for the Romans. They also took more than the government wanted, and kept the rest for themselves. Some became extremely rich. Their contact with Gentiles, and the fact that they often worked on the Sabbath, the Jewish holy day, made them ritually unclean, unfit to worship God.

Jesus' choice of Levi, then, is very shocking. Like the fishermen, Levi follows Jesus straight away. Mark shows that the Kingdom of God is for everybody, for outcasts like Levi, and those who eat with Jesus in the house as well.

The Pharisees, watching this, were extremely surprised.

The **Pharisees** were the largest religious party in Jesus' time. 'Pharisee' may mean 'someone who is separate from others'. They wanted to keep the Torah to the letter. Some Pharisees had normal jobs; others studied the Torah full time. They wanted to ensure that they did not break the least of the Torah's rules, even by accident. So they made extra rules to make sure its laws were never broken.

For example, the Torah said people should not work on the Sabbath. This was probably to give people a day off, for rest and worship. The Pharisees tried to define what 'work' meant, to make sure the command was not broken. They said 'work' included walking more than two-thirds of a mile. Even writing was classified as 'work'. Such rules became very difficult to keep.

19

The Pharisees also believed in ideas found in other parts of the Jewish Bible, such as angels, life after death, and the coming of the Messiah.

They would have been worried by Jesus' eating with people like Levi. Such people, they thought, were outcasts. Moreover, their food would not be kosher: it would not be the right type of food, prepared in the way set down in the Torah.

Jesus replies to their objections by saying it is people who are ill who need a doctor, not people who are well. The outcasts are included in the Kingdom, God's new society. Jews in Jesus' time sometimes pictured the Kingdom of God as a huge celebration meal: the Messianic Banquet. So, when Jesus eats with the tax collectors and sinners, it is a sign that they are being invited to the Messianic Banquet, the Kingdom of God.

The question about fasting
Read Mark 2.18-22

Strict Jews in Jesus' time fasted every Monday and Thursday from 6 a.m. to 6 p.m. This may explain why the disciples of John the Baptist and of the Pharisees were fasting.

The people who came to ask Jesus about this may well themselves have been Pharisees. Jesus says it is not the right time for fasting. It is a time to rejoice, just as the guests rejoice at a wedding. In the Old Testament, God was sometimes thought of as Israel's bridegroom. Mark again hints at Jesus' identity. The Old Testament prophet Hosea said that Israel's marriage to God had gone so wrong that there had been a divorce. But Hosea also predicted a new marriage. Jesus is the bridegroom in this new marriage between God and human beings.

A wedding feast also suggests the Messianic Banquet, the picture of the Kingdom of God as a celebration meal.

The bridegroom will be taken away: Jesus will die. After that, his followers will fast.

Jesus uses two images or parables to show that the new does not mix with the old. The Kingdom has replaced the old order of Judaism:

- it is no good patching an old coat with new cloth;
- wine which needs to ferment cannot be stored in brittle, used

20

wineskins: if it is, the skins will burst.

The Sabbath corn
Read Mark 2.23-28

Jews were allowed to pick food from fields or vineyards, so the disciples are not stealing. The Pharisees objected to it because the Law forbade work, including reaping, on the Sabbath (Exodus 34:21). Their interpretation of the Law is strict, as usual.

Jesus reminds them why God gave the Jews the Torah: to help them. After all, King David broke the Law by taking holy bread to eat when his men were hungry, and David was a great man of God. Human need comes before religious laws. Mark probably thinks that the Kingdom sits rather uneasily with Judaism.

Jesus says the Sabbath was made for people's benefit, not the other way round. He has the authority to say this because the Son of Man is Lord of the Sabbath. This outlook would have outraged these Pharisees. It was utterly alien to their way of thinking.

Revision tip:

Use the spot learning technique to learn what Jesus about the Sabbath. Again, it can help to learn one line at a time.

> The Sabbath was made for man;
> man was not made for the Sabbath.
> So the Son of Man is Lord
> even of the Sabbath.

Re-read the sections you need to know from Mark chapter 2, or listen to them on the CD.

Mark chapter 3

Jesus heals a man with a paralysed hand
Read Mark 3.1-6

Jewish laws allowed people to be healed on the Sabbath *but* this was only if life was in danger. The man in this story has a withered or paralysed hand, but he is not actually dying. The people who are waiting to see whether Jesus would do something wrong are the Pharisees from the previous incident (the controversy over the Sabbath corn).

Jesus puts human need above religious rules. The coming of the Kingdom means that the old rules are no longer so important. The importance of Jesus' healing on the Sabbath is not that it breaks the Law. Its importance is that it shows the Kingdom has come

The healing of many people
Read Mark 3.7-12

Another summary of Jesus healings, showing his compassion and that the Kingdom of God is on the way. The theme of the Messianic Secret continues: Jesus forbids the demons to identify him.

Jesus calls the Twelve
Read Mark 3.13-19

- The Old Testament speaks of the Jews, Israel, as the people of God. They were divided into twelve tribes.
- The new Israel, the new people of God, is those who are members of the Kingdom. At its core are the twelve disciples.

The disciples are also called 'apostles', which means 'those who are sent' or 'ambassadors'. They are to do three things:

1. To be with Jesus (as all Christians should be).
2. To preach. They are to spread the news about the Kingdom.
3. To drive out demons. This, again, is part of the work of the Messiah in bringing in the Kingdom. The disciples share in this work.

The disciples:
- are shown to be ordinary people;
- are led by Peter (next to Jesus);

- would become the later Christian leaders and some, including Peter and James, would die for their faith;
- are not perfect:
  - → James and John are called 'Boanerges' or 'sons (men) of thunder', possibly because of their quick tempers;
  - → Peter denied that he knew who Jesus was;
- were believed to have written some of the books and letters in the New Testament (1 and 2 Peter, John's Gospel, Matthew's Gospel);
- included Judas (we cannot be sure why Jesus chose the man who would betray him);
- included at least one Zealot: the second Simon. (Judas and possibly James and John may also have been Zealots.)

The **Zealots** (meaning 'fanatics') believed in fighting against the Romans. They believed their king should not be Caesar, but God or someone whom God would appoint: the Messiah, who would lead them in battle. The Romans thought of the Zealots as terrorists.

The fact that Jesus chose at least one Zealot as a disciple does not show he agreed with Zealots. It shows, again, that the Kingdom of God is for everybody.

Roman Catholic, Orthodox and most Anglican Christians believe bishops to be the successors of the Twelve. Roman Catholics believe the Pope to be the successor of Peter.

Jesus and Beelzebul
Read Mark 3.20-30

Jesus' family think he is 'beside himself': severely disturbed. The teachers of the Law (scribes) go further and say he is possessed by a demon. They think this gives him the power to perform exorcisms.

This idea is not just wicked, it is also stupid. If Jesus did use the Devil's power to drive out demons, then the forces of evil would be fighting among themselves, and God would still be winning.

Jesus' miracles are in fact signs of the Kingdom. The Devil, the 'strong man', is being tied up by the miracles and is being overthrown. The scribes' accusation comes very close to saying that something God does is not good at all, but evil. This sort of blindness makes forgiveness impossible. If people cannot recognize goodness when they see it, how can they turn to God and find forgiveness?

Jesus' mother and brothers
Read Mark 3.31-35

The point of this section is that anyone who does what God wants is in the Kingdom. They are as close to Jesus as the members of his own family.

Revision tip:

> *Re-read the sections you need to know from Mark 3.*
> *Then test your knowledge on them using the 'test yourself' questions at the end of this book.*

The Kingdom of God

Revision tip:

> *Every year, candidates throw marks away because they write 'the Kingdom of God means heaven.'*
> ***It doesn't!***
> *It's very important that you fully understand what is meant by 'the Kingdom of God';*
> *this is a very popular topic in exams and you need to learn it inside out,*
> *so it's worth coming back to this section of the book more than once.*

'The Kingdom of God' does not mean heaven, so what does it mean?
It's really all about God's rule: what happens when God's in charge.
Most Jews in Jesus' time were looking forward to this rule of God.
They were waiting for the Kingdom of God to arrive.

Revision tip:

> *Heaven can't 'arrive', so this reinforces that the Kingdom of God isn't heaven!*

The Jews had been ruled by foreign powers for many centuries. In 587BC, the Babylonians conquered Judah (the southern part of Israel), and their rule was followed by that of the Persians, then the Greeks, and finally the Romans.
The people began to hope for a time when *God* would be in charge, not another human empire. God would save them from their

enemies, just as he had long ago saved them from the Egyptians when Moses was their leader. Instead of just another human kingdom, the Kingdom of God would arrive.

The Kingdom of God, then, meant that God would be in charge. But different Jews had different ideas of the way in which God would rule:

- The Zealots thought the Kingdom of God meant that the Jews would rule their own country. Jewish rule was God's rule, so a Jewish kingdom would also be the Kingdom of God. Once he had defeated the Romans, the Messiah would be their king.
- The Essenes thought it meant there would be a war against the powers of darkness. All evil powers and evil people would be destroyed. The paradise that followed would be the Kingdom of God.

Jesus' teaching shows he disagreed with both these views. He believed in the Kingdom of God, but thought that **only God could bring it about**. Just as only God can make a seed grow, only he can make the Kingdom come (Mark 4: 26-29). **The Kingdom** would not involve a struggle against the Romans, but it **would involve a struggle against**:

1. **sin**, which Jesus forgives
2. **illness**, which Jesus heals
3. **demons**, whom Jesus defeats by exorcizing them (casting them out).

The Kingdom would also be a new society. It was not just about God ruling over the people, but also about the **people in the Kingdom**, the **members of the Kingdom of God**.

Also, the Kingdom was not just open to Jews. It was open to everybody. Sinners, outcasts and Gentiles could enter.

The relationship with God in the Kingdom was not just for this life: after death, people would be happy with God for ever. The future with Jesus, which would continue after death, is the full and final arrival of the Kingdom.

Note: in some of Jesus' sayings about the Kingdom, he appears to expect it to arrive in the future. In others, he speaks as though it is already here. Scholars have different views about Jesus' teaching on the Kingdom:

1. Some suggest Jesus did not think the Kingdom had *arrived*, but that it *would* arrive in the future, perhaps in the near future.

2. Others think he never said it would arrive in the future: it was *already here* in its fullness.

3. Others think Jesus taught that the Kingdom had *begun* with his coming, but that *it would arrive in its fullness later*. This is the view of the Kingdom taken by Mark's Gospel.

So,
everything Jesus says and does is somehow connected to the Kingdom:

The PARABLES teach about the nature of the Kingdom of God

The MIRACLES are performed on different sorts of people, who become members of the Kingdom of God:
children,
women,
outcasts,
Gentiles

People who are members of the Kingdom have their
SINS FORGIVEN by Jesus

If you become a member of the Kingdom now,
YOUR MEMBERSHIP WILL CONTINUE AFTER YOU HAVE DIED

JESUS' CLAIMS ABOUT HIMSELF
are claims about the Messiah,
who brings in the Kingdom of God

The arrival of the Kingdom means
OLD FASHIONED WAYS OF THINKING ARE NO LONGER SO IMPORTANT

Members of the Kingdom have to
BEHAVE IN A NEW WAY:
at the heart of this is loving their neighbours as themselves
(Mark 12.28-34)

Revision tip:

> *Read this section through again once more.*
> *Turn the book over.*
> *Write out bullet points on what you can remember of what you've read.*
> *Then check them against this section.*

Mark chapter 4

Revision tip:

> *Mark chapter 4 is a very popular area for exam questions.*

The parable of the sower and the purpose of the parables
Read Mark 4.1-20

Parables were stories used by teachers in Jesus' time. They got their point across by comparing one thing with another. Their imagery was usually drawn from people's everyday lives; Jesus' imagery often comes from farming.

Jesus' parables all teach about some aspect of the Kingdom of God.

The parable of the sower is unusual in that it is explained. Instead of the general picture being important, each part of the story represents something else. This type of parable is called an **allegory**.

The parable is interpreted as follows:

→ The sower = the person spreading God's word (translated as

27

'message' in the Good News Bible).

→ The seed that fell on the path, eaten by the birds = those who hear the word, but have it taken away by Satan.

→ The seed on rocky ground, which grows quickly and dries up = those who receive the word gladly, but who have no staying power: when trouble or persecution comes, they give up.

→ The seed sown among thorns, which is choked = those who are too attached to the world, who do not accept the message properly.

→ The seed sown among good soil which produces corn = those who hear and accept the word and who 'bear fruit'.

Nearly all scholars believe that the interpretation of the parable of the sower is not part of Jesus' original teaching. It has been added later by the early Christians: it has more to do with preaching the message of Christianity than with the coming of the Kingdom. Also, some of the vocabulary is more often found in early Christian writings than in Jesus' teaching (such as talk of persecution and calling the Christian message 'the word').

If this is right, then the original meaning of the parable seems to be that **the Kingdom will come, despite its small beginnings**.

God is like a farmer who sows seed everywhere. (This is what happened when you sowed seed by hand.) Some finds good soil, other seed does not. Yet the harvest of the Kingdom will come.

In verses 10-12, Jesus explains the purpose of the parables. For some people, they are riddles which are impossible to understand. People who have closed their minds remain outside the Kingdom: however hard they look, they will not understand anything. Jesus borrows some language from the prophet Isaiah to get this point across. The disciples, however, have been given the secret of the Kingdom. They may need to have some of the parables explained to them, but they are basically 'tuned in' to the Kingdom and will understand them.

It is possible that Mark thought Jesus deliberately wanted the parables to blind one group of people, who would remain outside the Kingdom. If so, Mark has missed the point. Parables were intended to make things easy to understand, not difficult.

Revision tip:

Make sure you know which category of seed corresponds to which type of person in the parable's explanation. It's worth drawing out a table to help you learn it.
Also, there are other parables in Mark 4 about plants growing. Don't confuse them with this one – lots of candidates do and it loses them marks!

More parables: 4.21-34

Revision tip:

Again, questions on these keep coming up in the exam. They have to be learnt really thoroughly.
Don't confuse them and make sure you know the less obvious ones too!
(Lots of candidates don't learn the seed growing secretly, for example, or mix it up with the sower.)

This is probably Mark's own collection of parables. Jesus would not have preached all of them on one occasion.

A lamp under a bowl
Read Mark 4:21-23

This shows:

what is hidden will be brought into the open:

Jesus' followers will see the Kingdom

the truth about the Kingdom needs to be brought into the open and spread.

Mark 4.24:

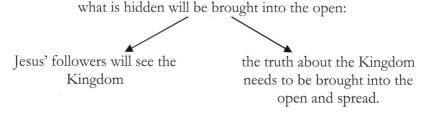

The measure you give will be the measure you get, and still more will be given you.

This is not easy. There are three possible meanings:
1. God will judge people after death in the same way as they have judged others. (This idea influences the Good News Bible translation. If you're using this translation, it's not good at all for this verse; best

29

ignore it and use the version above!)

2. Jesus is making the general comment that we get out of life what we put into it. (This is unlikely: it has nothing to do with the Kingdom of God.)

3. Jesus is again speaking of the Kingdom. If people are 'tuned in' to the Kingdom, their understanding will increase.

Mark 4.25:

> For to him who has will more be given;
> and from him who has not,
> even what he has will be taken away.

This seems to mean that if you are already 'tuned in' to the parables, you will understand things even better. If your mind is closed, you will end up worse than you were in the first place. This could apply to the legalism of the Pharisees.

Revision tip:

The two quotations in speech bubbles are worth learning.
Again, spot memory techniques will help.

The parable of the growing seed
Read Mark 4.26-29

This is the second parable of growth; the first was the parable of the sower.

Scholars used to think that these parables show that the Kingdom arrives gradually, just as a seed gradually turns into a plant. This rather misses the point. It is not important how long the process takes: the important thing is that the plant actually does appear. People will see that the Kingdom has come.

It is not clear who the farmer represents:

- If he represents God, God lets the world run on, and then brings in the harvest of the Kingdom.
- If, as seems more likely, the farmer represents Jesus' followers, their

job is to sow the seed (the message) and then leave it to God to bring in the Kingdom. The Kingdom cannot be brought about by human actions, as the Zealots thought.

The parable of the mustard seed
Read Mark 4.30-32

This is another parable of growth. It shows that the Kingdom will come as surely as a tiny seed grows into a huge plant. Jesus' work may seem to have little effect at the moment, but the Kingdom will arrive. In the Old Testament, 'birds' sometimes meant foreigners. The parable may be saying that foreigners (Gentiles) will be included in the Kingdom.

Why Jesus used parables
Read Mark 4.33-34

The passage shows that Jesus told other parables which Mark does not include. The reason Mark gives is similar to that in 4.10-12.

Jesus calms a storm
Read Mark 4.35-41

This is one of the 'nature miracles', so called because they show Jesus' power over the forces of nature. The other nature miracles are the walking on the water, the feeding of the five thousand, the feeding of the four thousand and the cursing of the fig-tree.

The Sea of Galilee is still a stormy place. Yet the meaning of the story is more than Jesus simply stopping a violent storm: it shows who Jesus is.

God is shown to have power over water in the Old Testament:
- He parted the waters of the Red Sea to allow his people through when they fled from Egypt (Exodus 14). In the Psalms, sailors in trouble called on God, and he 'made the storm be still, and the waves of the sea were hushed' (Psalm 107.29). The Jews believed that God controlled the weather. So, **Jesus behaves as though he is God.**

When God did something extraordinary in the Old Testament,

people were said to be frightened.

- For example, when God gave Moses the Ten Commandments, the people 'trembled with fear' at the signs of God's appearing on the mountain. So, **the disciples were afraid because they were seeing God at work.**

It also shows Mark's readers how to live. Christians in distress should trust in Jesus' power to save them, not panic as the disciples did. If Mark's first readers were being persecuted by Nero, they should trust in Christ even in the face of death.

It is interesting that Mark is not afraid to show the disciples in a bad light. They are annoyed with Jesus here for sleeping, and they have very little faith in him.

Jesus as saviour

The title 'saviour' is not one Jesus used for himself but it is commonly applied to him by Christians today. In fact, the name 'Jesus' is linked to the word 'saviour'.

'Jesus' is the English version of his name; historically, he was actually called Yeshua, the Aramaic form of 'Jesus'. Another English version of Yeshua is Joshua. And the name means 'God saves'.

Mark shows Jesus to be the saviour in four ways:
1. by showing that Jesus saves people from illness and evil;
2. by showing that Jesus gives people all they need (the feeding miracles show this);
3. by showing that Jesus saves people in danger (the calming of the storm and the walking on the water show this);

– and, most importantly:

4. by the story on Jesus' suffering, death and resurrection.

Revision tip:

It's very important that you learn the set texts in Mark 4 very thoroughly. It's easy to get confused between the parables and this loses people marks. Keep going over the text of Mark 4 until you know it; it's best to do this little and often rather than trying to cram it all in at one sitting. Try using a variety of methods: read the text, listen to the CD, and use the test yourself questions at the back of this book. For the shorter parables and sayings in Mark 4.21-32, it's worth writing each one out on cue cards, slipping them into your pocket, and referring to them at odd moments during the day. Or, again, use spot learning techniques. Illustrating the cue cards with little pictures may sound silly but it will help you to learn the texts.

Mark chapter 5

The madman in the tombs
Read Mark 5.1-20

Another exorcism story, very vividly told. The man is possessed by as many demons as there are soldiers in a Roman legion. Hence he gives his name as Legion ('Mob' in the Good News Bible). The miracle takes place at Gerasa or Gadara (different Greek copies of Mark give both names). Neither of these places is very near the Sea of Galilee, which shows that Mark's geography is not very good. However, it is important that they are both Gentile towns. The man Jesus heals is a Gentile; Gentiles are admitted into the Kingdom.

Legion is chained up in a region near some tombs, one of the locations where it was believed demons lived. Mark thinks the demons give him the supernatural insight to recognize Jesus. Jesus asks him his name: it was believed that an exorcist could cast out a demon more easily if he knew his name. The destruction of the pigs demonstrates that the demons have been cast out.

After he is cured, the man spreads the message about Jesus throughout the Gentile region of the Ten Towns (the Decapolis).

Some scholars have suggested that a miracle story about Jesus has been mixed up with a folk tale about some pigs. This is possible, but there is no real evidence. A more conservative view is that that Legion needed proof that he was cured, so Jesus somehow made the pigs stampede, or they ran off when they were frightened by the madman.

Jairus' daughter and the woman who touched Jesus' cloak
Read Mark 5.21-43

Both these stories involve females. Women and girls were considered to be second-class citizens in the Jewish world of Jesus' day. However, Jesus does not share this attitude. If someone needs help, it is given. It does not matter whether that person is male or female.

The woman who touched Jesus' cloak had a menstrual problem, or some infection that produced similar symptoms. This would have made her unclean according to the Torah, but her faith, Jesus says, has 'saved' her (this is what the Greek says). She is completely cured, in body, mind and spirit. She is now one of the family, a 'daughter' of Jesus and a member of the Kingdom of God.

Jairus organized the worship in the local synagogue. He too has faith in Jesus, who takes Peter, James and John with him. These three disciples are the only ones present at some other important events, including the Transfiguration and the visit to Gethsemane.

This is the only miracle story in Mark in which Jesus raises the dead. It is therefore very important:

- Only God has power over death. In the Old Testament, Elijah prays that God will bring a dead boy back to life, and God does so. But here Jesus does not pray first: he does it himself. **Again, Jesus behaves as though he is God.**
- Jesus' raising the little girl from death is a shadow of what is to come at the end of Mark: Jesus will himself rise from the dead. (However, Jairus' daughter was brought back to normal life, whereas Jesus was raised to a new kind of life.)
- **The story reminds the readers that Jesus will save them from death as well.** Christians' relationship with Jesus in the Kingdom will, they believe, continue after death.

Revision tip:

Review all the set texts you need from Mark chapters 1 to 5. Read them through carefully or listen to them on CD.

Mark chapter 6

Jesus is rejected at Nazareth
Read Mark 6.1-6

Jesus has been carrying on his mission for some time before he goes home. The people of Nazareth want to hear what he has to say for himself, so they go to the synagogue. Yet they all know his family, and they cannot believe that their carpenter is anything special.

Jesus says that a prophet is welcome everywhere except at home, by his own people. This was a well-known proverb. They have no faith in Jesus or in the Kingdom. So Jesus can do nothing for them, except for a few healings. God can do nothing for people who do not want him.

Jesus sends out the Twelve
Read Mark 6.7-13

In their mission, the Twelve must:

- preach that people should 'repent'. More than just 'be sorry', this means turn away from their sins, completely change their outlook and lifestyle;
- drive out demons;
- heal the sick.

All this shares in Jesus' work of bringing in the Kingdom of God. Mark thinks that the Church, following on from the disciples, also shares in this work of Jesus.

The disciples are to travel light: they are to be completely dependent on God. They can take sandals and a stick, but no money, beggar's bowl, food or extra clothes. They must not stay anywhere too long or waste time on people who will not listen to them. They are not to beg, because wandering preachers in Jesus' time were sometimes dishonest.

Jews returning from Gentile towns would shake the dust from their feet. The disciples must now do it for *Jewish* towns where people will not listen. Mark thinks times have changed. It no longer matters whether or not you are a Jew. What matters is whether or not you accept the apostles' teaching about the Kingdom. By shaking dust off their shoes, the apostles are warning people that they could be left outside the Kingdom.

The instructions to the disciples may also have been used by later Christian missionaries, perhaps in Mark's own time.

The death of John the Baptist
Read Mark 6.14-29

The story starts with the theme, 'Who is Jesus?' People get the answer wrong: he is not John, he is not Elijah and he is not a prophet. He is greater than any of these.

The story of John's death, which is also told by the Jewish historian Josephus, is fairly straightforward. Herod Antipas ruled Galilee for the Romans. Strictly speaking, he was not a king, but a tetrarch (ruler). His family had a reputation for immorality. John spoke out against Herod and it cost him his life.

The feeding of the five thousand
Read Mark 6.30-44

The Old Testament says that, when Moses was their leader, God fed his people in the desert with food from heaven called manna. The feeding of the five thousand also takes place in a desert.

One Jewish teacher (rabbi) said that the Messiah would feed people miraculously as Moses had done. In the Old Testament, too, Elijah's successor Elisha fed one hundred men with twenty small loaves (2 Kings 4: 42-44).

So, the story shows:
1.   Jesus is the Messiah who feeds the people as Moses had done.
2.   Jesus fulfils the Law, represented by Moses, and the prophets, represented by Elisha.
3.   Jesus behaves as though he is God.

The story also looks forward to the Last Supper and to the Messianic Banquet. (The Messianic Banquet was an image of the Kingdom as a big celebratory meal.) The Messiah here hosts a meal for a lot of people, just as he will at the Messianic Banquet. He gives the people bread, just as he will give the disciples the bread of his body at the Last Supper, and the Church – Mark's Church, and the Church today – will repeat his actions in the Eucharist.

Some scholars have suggested that the whole story has been invented, or that the number of people or the amount of food has been exaggerated, or that people just shared their packed lunch, and this was mistaken for a miracle. Not everyone finds these 'explanations' very convincing. Certainly Mark thought he was writing about a miracle, and a very important one at that. He gives us two versions of it: there is also the feeding of the four thousand in 8.1-10.

The walking on the water
Read Mark 6.45-52

Another nature miracle.

Again, it hints at who Jesus is by mentioning his power over the water and the disciples' fear. See the notes on 'Jesus calms a storm'.

In the Old Testament, God is also pictured as walking over the sea in Psalm 77.19: 'Your way was through the sea, your path, through the mighty waters.'

Jesus is said to be about to 'pass by' the disciples. These words are also found in the Old Testament: God 'passed by' Moses and Elijah in the books of Exodus and 1 Kings.

Jesus also calls out to his disciples, 'It is I.' The Greek words Mark uses here are simply, 'I am', which is what God calls himself in Exodus 3.14. So, once again, Jesus behaves as though he is God.

Some have attempted to explain away the story by saying Jesus was walking on a reef, or had built a raft. Neither of these are very convincing. Others suggest it was made up to fit in with the Old Testament. Still others point out that if God made the universe, he is not going to find it hard to make Jesus walk on water!

The feeding miracles had pointed to Jesus' identity. That is why the disciples were said not to understand about the 'loaves' (the Good News Bible makes this clearer by saying 'they had not understood the real meaning of the feeding of the five thousand'). The disciples did not work out who Jesus was from the feeding miracles, and they still cannot grasp it.

Another summary of Jesus' healings
Read Mark 6.53-56

The summaries of the healings show that Jesus' miracles were not just the few that Mark selects. Jesus is shown to have had a huge reputation as a miracle worker.

In this third summary of the healings, Jesus' power is so great that people only have to touch the edge of his clothes to be cured.

Mark chapter 7

What makes a person unclean?
Read Mark 7.1-23

Mark explains the Pharisees' rules on ceremonial washing, for the benefit of his Gentile readers. The Pharisees thought these traditions were nearly as important as the Torah itself.

The Pharisees expect the disciples to wash their hands in the traditional way. (This was to do with ritual, not with hygiene.) Jesus says they are the hypocrites of whom Isaiah spoke. They have fallen into the trap of thinking their own tradition is as important as what God wants.

This can be seen in Corban laws. One of the Ten Commandments is 'honour your father and mother'. This would obviously cover looking after them, which could cost money. People could get out of spending money on their needy parents, however, by making a solemn oath that the cash 'belonged to God': it was 'Corban'. They broke God's Law by taking advantage of a man-made rule.

Jesus' words in verse 15 area real bombshell. The Pharisees are completely wrong. Nothing that goes into someone can make them 'unclean' or ceremonially impure. God is not really bothered about how people wash their hands, or whether they keep strict kosher rules. What really matters is what comes from the heart: the evil things that come from within.

One of the biggest issues that faced the early Church was whether Gentile Christians had to keep the Torah. Mark's Church was probably Gentile; stories like this were useful in the debate. Since Mark includes this account, it is likely that the debate was still going on when he was writing.

Jesus heals a Gentile woman's daughter
Read Mark 7.24-30

Most Jews in Jesus' time thought women were second-class citizens. They would have thought Gentile women were even worse! Jesus once again treats people as people, regardless of their sex or race.

Jesus says it is unfair to take bread from the children (Jews) and throw it to the dogs (Gentiles). (He was certainly not being insulting, which would be completely out of character, but most likely joking ironically.) The woman from Syro-Phoenicia is very sharp, and replies that even the dogs under the table get the children's scrap. Her faith is great, and Jesus cures her daughter. It is interesting that he does so from a distance.

The woman calls Jesus 'Lord' ('sir' in some translations). Both 'Lord' and 'sir' translate the Greek word *kyrios* into English. Any man with authority could be called *kyrios*. It was also the name used for God in the Greek translation of the Old Testament. **The title 'Lord' shows that Jesus has authority, and also hints at who he really is.**

Jesus heals a deaf-mute
Read Mark 7.31-37

Another Gentile healing. There are other stories of healers in the ancient world who used saliva in their cures. (This may be why the other Gospels omit this story.) Mark gives Jesus' words of healing in Aramaic, the language Jesus spoke, and translates them for his non-Jewish readers. He may have got them from Peter, and may include them for the benefit of Christian healers who believed they needed to use such words.

The passage is similar to Isaiah's prediction that when the Messiah came, the blind would be able to see, and the deaf hear.

Mark chapter 8

The feeding of the four thousand
Read Mark 8.1-10

The notes on the feeding of the five thousand (p.36) are relevant here. It is almost certainly a different version of the same story.

The feeding of the four thousand takes place in the region of the Ten Towns or Decapolis, a Gentile area. The feeding of the five thousand took place in Jewish area. So,

• the feeding of the four thousand shows the bread of life being given to the Gentiles;

- the feeding of the five thousand shows the bread of life being given to the Jews.

Both Jews and Gentiles take part in a meal which is a shadow of the Messianic Banquet. Both are therefore included in the Kingdom of God.

The Pharisees ask for a sign; the yeast of the Pharisees and of Herod
Read Mark 8.11-21

Throughout his work Jesus has been giving signs by performing miracles. Yet the Pharisees still want a sign. They refuse to see what has been staring them in the face, and will not believe.

Jesus refuses to do a miracle solely for their benefit. Even if he did, they would probably still not accept it.

The next few verses (14-21) are difficult. Jesus warns the disciples against the 'yeast' of the Pharisees and of Herod. The rabbis sometimes used the word 'yeast' to mean evil intentions or ideas. Jesus is warning the Twelve against the Pharisees' teaching, and perhaps against the followers of Herod Antipas.

The disciples think he is complaining because they have forgotten their packed lunches. They ought to know better by now: they have seen the two feeding miracles, so they should realize that they can rely on Jesus.

It is difficult to be sure why Jesus reminds the disciples about the number of baskets. It may be because twelve is a number associated with the Jews (twelve tribes of Israel). Seven is a 'Gentile number' (there were seven deacons or Church leaders in Acts to look after the Gentiles; the Gentile world was also divided into seventy countries, and $7 \times 10 = 70$). Both Jews and Gentiles were fed by Jesus, and both were included in the Kingdom of God. Jesus drives this point home by talking about the number of baskets.

The blind man at Bethsaida
Read Mark 8.22-26

This miracle is very similar to the healing of the deaf-mute. Again, the same points need to be noted. In both, the man's friends ask for

Jesus' help, he uses saliva, and tries to keep his Messiahship secret. This story is unusual because the cure happens gradually, not immediately.

Jesus opens a blind man's eyes. In the stories which follow this one, he opens his disciples' eyes to who he really is.

Peter's declaration about Jesus
Read Mark 8.27-9.1

Before this point in the Gospels, the disciples have not said who they think Jesus is. Indeed, they have often been very confused. Some people have been saying Jesus is John the Baptist, Elijah, or another prophet.

Near Caesarea Philippi, Jesus asks them who they say he is. Peter replies that Jesus is the Christ (Messiah).

This is the right answer, but they must keep it to themselves. They and others must learn what the Messiah is to do: he is to suffer, die and to rise again.

Note: Jesus refers to himself here as the Son of Man, not such a loaded title as 'Messiah'. Nobody expected the Messiah to die a criminal's death, let alone rise again. Peter certainly cannot take it in, so he tells Jesus off. Jesus angrily calls him 'Satan': the one who tempts people to do wrong.

Jesus then teaches the crowd what it means to follow him:

- They must be prepared to give up everything, and follow him to the death if necessary: to take up their cross.

- Those who do not want to do this, but prefer to cling to worldly things, will lose the most precious thing they have: themselves. People will find themselves fully in giving up everything for Jesus and for the gospel. Nothing can buy back a ruined and worthless life.

- Those who are ashamed of Jesus will find he is ashamed of them at his second coming.

- Some will not die before they see that the Kingdom of God has come. (This, 9.1, is a very difficult verse. It may mean that they will realize that the Kingdom is already here with Jesus. Or it may refer to the Transfiguration, which follows 9.1, or to the resurrection. Or it may show that some, perhaps including Jesus himself, thought the second coming would happen soon.)

Jesus also predicts his suffering and death in 9.30-32 and 10.32-34. It is worth reading these verses. In the first passage, the disciples do not understand and are too afraid to ask. They remain very frightened in the second.

Peter calls Jesus **'the Christ'** (= **'the Messiah'**) in this story. It is important to remember some information about this title:

- Messiah (Hebrew) and Christ (Greek) should both be translated as 'the anointed one'. In the Old Testament, kings were anointed. Therefore the Messiah was the king.

- The ancient kings of Israel were often less than ideal. In 587 BC, the last king to be descended from the great King David was deposed by the Babylonians, and there were none after him. These two things made the Jews hope for an ideal king: the Messiah.

- In Jesus' time, many thought the Messiah would be a warrior who would throw the Romans out of Israel.

- The Essenes expected two (perhaps three) Messiahs. One would be a priest, the other a king.

- Jesus rejected his contemporaries' views. The Messiah's job was not to win a war, but to suffer, die and rise again.

Additional material about Peter's declaration from Matthew's Gospel (Matthew 16.13-20)

Not all exam boards set this passage, so please ignore this section if your specification does not include it.

Matthew used Mark as one of his major sources, yet his version of Peter's declaration has more material. Jesus' reaction to Peter is much less cool here than it is in Mark. While Mark goes straight to the command to keep quiet, Matthew has Jesus telling Peter he is the foundation of the Church.

Matthew is clearly using another source for verses 16-19. Whether Mark knew this material is unknown.

Matthew's version of the incident is particularly important to Roman Catholic Christians.

In fact, most Christians are Roman Catholic. It's hard to be certain of the figures, but good estimates say it's around 59% of the total. So why does this passage matter so much to them?

We need to consider some background here; it's to do with the way leadership in the Churches is structured.

A leadership structure emerged early in Christian history. It is sometimes called the 'three-fold ministry'. In the second century, it was firmly in place. There are three types of Christian leaders:

- Bishops
- Priests
- Deacons

The Roman Catholic Church has this structure. So does the Anglican Church (which includes the Church of England, the Church of Wales and the Church of Ireland) and the Orthodox Church.

Bishops run the Church in each *diocese,* an administrative area about the size of a county. The assistants to the bishop, who work on a more local level, are the **priests** and the **deacons**. **The bishop is usually believed to be a successor to Jesus' original twelve disciples or apostles.** (This is called the doctrine of the *'apostolic succession'.*) Because of this, bishops are very important; Roman Catholics especially listen carefully to what their bishops teach. The bishop of Rome is called the **Pope**.

So, back to the section in Matthew. Jesus tells Peter he is the foundation for the Church: the rock, in fact. The Greek for 'rock' is *petros,* and this is also the Greek form of the name 'Peter'. Simon's name was changed to Petros / Peter by Jesus.

The Church, built on Peter, will never be conquered by Hades. This was the underworld in Greek mythology; it's usually translated as 'hell' here. The Church, the people of God, will always survive. Peter's given the keys to the Kingdom of Heaven; Matthew tends to use this term rather than 'Kingdom of God' but it means the same thing.

We know that Peter went on to lead the Christian community in Rome. The Roman Catholic teaching is that he was the first bishop of Rome, the first Pope, and that every Pope since then is the successor of Peter himself. Moreover, the authority Jesus gives to Peter is passed on to his successors too. Peter was the most important of the apostles. Peter's successor, the Pope, is the most important of the apostles' successors, the bishops.

Jesus gives Peter the authority to make decisions, to bind and loose. For Roman Catholics, the Pope has this authority too. His teaching work is very important, and Catholics have a duty to listen to what the Pope says. They can find out what he teaches through the media, and through letters called encyclicals, which the Pope writes on various subjects.

(Anglicans and the Orthodox accept the Pope is the Bishop of Rome. They don't, though, accept other claims Roman Catholics make about him; they would not usually accept that he has a special role in teaching Christians, for example.)

Jesus also tells Peter, 'Whatever you bind on earth will be bound in heaven, and whatever you loose on earth will be loosed in heaven.' This is similar to what the risen Jesus says to the disciples in John 20.23: 'If you forgive anyone's sins, they are forgiven; if you retain anyone's sins, they are retained.'

Both passages are taken by most Christians today to refer to the **sacrament of**

reconciliation (also called **confession**). This sacrament is found in the Roman Catholic, Anglican and Orthodox Churches. Bishops and their assistants the priests can forgive people's sins in Jesus' name. In the sacrament of reconciliation, someone tells a priest what they have done, and, if they're genuinely sorry, they receive Jesus' forgiveness from the priest. The process is done in absolute confidence; the priest is not allowed in any circumstances whatsoever to tell anyone else what was said.

So, Matthew's version of Peter's confession is very important for most Christians today:

- **For the Roman Catholic Church, the authority Jesus gives Peter is passed on to his successors, the Popes.**
- **For the Roman Catholic, Orthodox and Anglican Church, the power to bind and loose is applied to the sacrament of reconciliation, or confession.**

Revision tip:

Re-read the set texts from Mark chapters 6-8. As you do so, jot down a few bullet points (no more than five) about what the texts say, under the headings 'Townspeople in Nazareth', 'Disciples', 'Miracles', 'Pharisees', 'Corban', and 'Who is Jesus?'
This is an active reading exercise; making the notes helps to concentrate your mind on the texts.
So, they don't need to be complete or thorough and you don't need to refer to them again.

Mark chapter 9

The Transfiguration
Read Mark 9.2-13

The story of the Transfiguration shows Peter, James and John who Jesus really is. The account is like a code, which can be cracked:

It takes place on a **mountain** ⟶	In the Old Testament (OT), mountains symbolize closeness to God
Jesus is **transfigured** and his clothes become dazzling **white** ⟶	Angels and God in the OT are pictured as wearing white, so the human Jesus is also the Son of God
The disciples are **afraid** ⟶	Fear is the reaction in the OT to an appearance of God (a *theophany*)
Peter wants to make **3 tents** ⟶	The Jewish festival of Tabernacles recalled how the people lived in tents in the desert

when Moses was leader. There was even a tent-shrine for God, who was particularly close to them. Peter thinks the time has come when God, in Jesus, will once again dwell with his people. But you cannot stick God's glory in a tent. God's glory is in Jesus, and in Jesus' work.

The **voice** repeats the words at the baptism and says that Jesus is the Son of God ⟶	People are to **listen to** Jesus. Jesus has just taught and will teach again that he must **suffer.**
Elijah, the greatest prophet, and **Moses** appear ⟶	The Jews thought Elijah would arrive before the Messiah. Moses had predicted that God would send the people a new prophet. Elijah and Moses both suffered for their faith and the Son of God must also suffer. Jesus implies that Elijah did come before the Messiah arrived, but as John the Baptist.

Revision tip:

Draw a sketch or cartoon of what happened at the Transfiguration. This is a revision exercise so it does not have to be a brilliant picture. Label the features and what they mean / why they're important (e.g. the mountain, white clothes, Elijah, Moses).

Jesus heals an epileptic boy
Read Mark 9.14-29

The boy's symptoms suggest that he has epilepsy, which was attributed to a very violent demon. Jesus performs a miracle in healing the boy. Note that there is no cure for epilepsy, even today.

A major theme of the story is **the need for faith**. Here, the teachers of the Law (scribes) have no faith. The disciples need it: they have been given the authority to heal people, but Mark probably thinks they cannot do so here because of their lack of faith. The boy's father needs greater faith. His outburst in verse 24 has provided an apt prayer for Christians in difficult times. It may have been especially important to Mark's own Church, if it was persecuted by Nero.

Jesus says only **prayer** can cast out this sort of demon.

Who is the greatest?
Read Mark 9.33-37

The disciples' dispute about which of them is the greatest is resolved by Jesus' saying, 'Whoever wants to be first must be last of all and servant of all.' This is the way Jesus himself behaves.

Children are dependent and need to be looked after. If the disciples want to be great, they should help those who need to be looked after. If they welcome a child in Jesus' name, they are welcoming Jesus. If they welcome Jesus, they are welcoming God.

Being in the Kingdom is not about status or power; it is about serving others.

Some teachings of Jesus
Read Mark 9.38-50

'Whoever is not against us is for us' (9.38-41) shows that the disciples should not be too possessive about their authority. They should not have told off the exorcist who did not belong to their group. After all, such outsiders could become followers of Jesus. The disciples should remember that anyone who does no more than give them a cup of water because they bear Christ's name will be rewarded.

'Temptations to sin' (9.42-48) warns that some things people do will result in their being sent to hell. 'Hell' is the English word for Gehenna, which was a rubbish dump outside Jerusalem. The burning rubbish made it an effective symbol for the place where evil people would be punished after death.

Jesus is saying that if you cause someone, including yourself, to stumble, you will be punished. 'Stumble' may mean 'lose faith' (as the Good News Bible translates it) or it may mean 'sin'.

It is a terrible fate to be drowned with a millstone around your neck. Yet it is even more terrible to cause 'one of these little ones' (either children or simply 'Christians') to stumble.

Jesus also warns his followers not to let themselves stumble. They should want the life of the Kingdom. It is far more important even than a hand, or a foot, or an eye.

'Salt' (verses 49-50): a difficult passage. It may mean that Christians should be pure, or that they may have to suffer the fire of persecution.

If Christians lose their purity, they will be no use to anyone.

Revision tip:
About an hour after studying these passages, go back and read again the set texts from Mark 9. Then test your knowledge with the 'test yourself' questions at the back of this book.

Mark chapter 10

Jesus' teaching on divorce
Read Mark 10.1-12

The Torah did not allow a woman to divorce her husband, but a man could divorce his wife if she were 'guilty of some shameful conduct' (Deuteronomy 24.1). The issue was: how 'shameful' did the 'conduct' have to be?

Jews in Jesus' time were divided into two schools of thought:

* Some who agreed with Rabbi Shammai: 'shameful conduct' meant adultery and nothing else.
* More who agreed with Rabbi Hillel: 'shameful conduct' meant anything the man did not like. He could therefore divorce his wife if she burnt his dinner or had got old and he no longer liked her looks.

Divorce for a woman was a terrible disgrace. Given all this, it is hardly surprising that Jesus is so strict. The Torah allowed divorce only because human beings were pig-headed. Yet when God created them, they were designed for marriage. There should therefore be no divorce. Re-marriage is adultery.

(Jesus mentions women divorcing their husbands because this was allowed by Roman law.)

Jesus is saying that women should be allowed to live in love, security and respect.

Christians today have differing views on divorce:

* Some think it is always wrong. The Roman Catholic Church does not recognise divorce at all. However, it does allow 'annulment'. This is a declaration, in certain cases, that a marriage never took place.

- Others allow divorce, even though nobody thinks it is ideal. In Matthew's Gospel, Jesus does seem to allow it if adultery has taken place, and Jesus says his teaching on marriage 'does not apply to everyone, but only to those to whom God has given it' (Matthew 19.11). Some would argue that taking a hard line with people in difficult and distressing circumstances is not the best way to help them. Divorce and remarriage is permitted by the Anglican Church, the Orthodox and by most Protestant Churches.

Jesus blesses the children
Read Mark 10.13-16

The Kingdom of God belongs to people like children. Children can be seen as eager to learn, trusting and loving. This is the way Christians should be towards God.

But children are of course not always like this, so the point seems to be wider. Children in Jesus' day had little social standing, so the Kingdom of God belongs to others like them: the poor, the oppressed and the outcasts.

Those who do not receive the Kingdom of God like a child will not enter it. Children generally do not turn their noses up at things done especially for them. The disciples should have this child-like openness towards the gift of the Kingdom.

The rich man
Read Mark 10.17-31

It was good that the rich man kept the rules of the Torah, but his money was stopping him getting closer to God. The Jewish view was that money was a gift from God. So the disciples were amazed: if it is going to be hard for the rich to enter the Kingdom, it is going to be even harder for the poor!

But this misses the point. The coming of the Kingdom changes things. The Kingdom is the most important thing there is and nothing must get in the way: money, or even family and friends. People who give everything up for the Kingdom will be rewarded with new 'brothers', 'sisters' and 'mothers' among their fellow-Christians in the Church, and also with eternal life.

People cannot enter the Kingdom by their own efforts. It is easier to push a camel through the eye of a needle than to squeeze a rich person into God's Kingdom. But then nothing is impossible for God.

In the Kingdom, the tables will be turned. Many of the first will be last, and many of the last will be first. Those whom the world thinks are the most important will be the last to squeeze into the Kingdom, and will not be the most important in it. But those whom the world thinks are the least important will be the first into the Kingdom, and perhaps the most important people in it as well.

(The correct attitude to wealth is shown in the story of the widow's mite; see Mark 12.41-44.)

Jesus said to the rich man, 'sell what you have and give to the poor.' This certainly shows that Christians should care for the poor. But did Jesus mean that everybody should give away all their possessions? Is it bad to be rich?

Possible answers:

- Jesus was talking to one man. He did not mean everybody.
- Money is only bad if you make it into an idol. However, if you have money you should use it to help others.
- Only some people have the strength to do what Jesus told the rich man to do. Hence monks and nuns take a vow of poverty and live without their own possessions.
- Christians should share their possessions, as did the earliest Christians in the Acts of the Apostles. Christians simply fail to live up to the standards Jesus set.

Jesus predicts his suffering and resurrection
Read Mark 10.32-34

This is more detailed than the other predictions of the Passion (from the Greek word for 'to suffer'). Jesus strides ahead of the disciples, who are 'amazed' and 'afraid': he has the courage to face what is ahead.

James' and John's question
Read Mark 10.35-45

James and John want positions of power in the Kingdom. Again, they

49

have missed the point. The Kingdom is not about power but about service.

If the Messiah's job is to suffer and die to redeem many, then his disciples should be ready to suffer for others. They should be ready to share the cup and the baptism of Jesus' suffering.

James and John did remain faithful to Jesus. James was executed for his faith, though in fact it seems that John lived to a great age.

Mark's readers would have been reminded here of the cup used at the Eucharist, and of their own baptism. Both are linked to suffering. Mark may well be reminding his readers, who may have been persecuted by Nero, what their faith means.

Jesus cannot grant favours to his friends: the Father has already decided who is to have the chief places in the Kingdom. They will certainly not go to bigheads who want power. The most important people in the Kingdom are those who do most to help others: 'The Son of Man also came not to be served but to serve, and to give his life as a ransom for many.'

Jesus heals blind Bartimaeus
Read Mark 10.46-50

Jericho was only fifteen miles from Jerusalem. Jesus and the disciples are on a journey, and now very near to the place where he will die. It is the disciples who are really blind, not Bartimaeus. This healing follows on from James' and John's question. The disciples still do not understand what Jesus' mission means. They need to follow Jesus, just as Bartimaeus follows him on the road. That road leads to Jerusalem and to Golgotha.

The title **Son of David** for Jesus is only found twice in Mark: here, and in the passage with the question about the Messiah (12.35-37). David was the great Jewish king who, a thousand years before Jesus, was promised by God that one of his descendants or 'sons' would always rule (2 Samuel 7.12-13). 'Son of David' means 'descendant of David' and was another name for the Messiah.

Revision tip:
  Go back over all the set texts in Mark 6-10, either reading them or using the CD.

Mark chapter 11

The triumphal entry
Read Mark 11.1-11

Jesus enters Jerusalem, and the Passion story begins. 'Passion' comes from a Greek word meaning 'to suffer'.

The people greet Jesus as the Messiah. The Old Testament prophet Zechariah had predicted that the Messiah would arrive at Jerusalem, 'humble' and 'riding on a donkey' (Zechariah 9.9). Jesus fulfils this prophecy. Victorious kings used to ride war horses in processions. Jesus rides on a colt because he has come in peace.

The crowd's greeting, 'Blessed is he who comes in the name of the Lord!' was the normal greeting for any pilgrim who arrived in Jerusalem. Passover time was near, and people were flocking to the holy city. Yet they also recognize that the Kingdom is near.

The word 'Hosanna' originally meant 'save now'. By Jesus' time, it had become a traditional shout of praise.

Jesus' triumphal entry into Jerusalem is remembered by Christians today on **Palm Sunday**, the first day of **Holy Week**. Holy Week is the last week of Lent, the forty day period which prepares Christians for Easter. On Palm Sunday, Christians often re-enact Jesus' entry into Jerusalem, usually during the Eucharist. There may be a procession, with palm branches or palm crosses (crosses made from palm leaves). The hymns and readings remember the welcome the crowd gave Jesus, and the rest of his Passion.

The cursing of the fig- tree
Read Mark 11.12-14 and 20-25

Some find this story totally out of character, and cannot believe Jesus did it. Others have suggested that a parable told by Jesus has been turned into a story about him. Mark probably thinks of it as an acted prophecy: a visual aid. Some of the Old Testament prophets performed symbolic actions to get a message across, as Jesus does here.

The fig-tree in the Old Testament was used as a symbol for Israel (Jeremiah 8.13). So the story's interpretation is as follows:

51

Jesus is hungry for figs.	⟶	God is 'hungry' for the 'fruit' of good actions and true religion from Israel.
It is not the right time for figs.	⟶	It is not the right time for God to gain 'fruit' from his people.
No one will ever eat from the tree again.	⟶	The fig tree of Israel is also barren. The new Israel of the Kingdom has replaced it.
The fig tree dies.	⟶	The time of Israel as God's people is over.

Mark places some of Jesus' teaching on prayer after this story. This shows that he also sees the miracle as a sign of the power of faith.

The idea that you can move mountains if you have enough faith is not to be taken literally. It means that you will be able to overcome problems and hardships that seemed impossible.

God will always answer people's prayers, but people will also have to forgive others when they pray. If they do not, they cannot receive forgiveness for their own sins.

The cleansing of the Temple
Read Mark 11.15-19

Jesus is now in Jerusalem. This incident and all the following passages are set in Holy Week, the week leading up to his death. The story is framed by the cursing of the fig-tree and the theme is the same.

The Old Testament prophet Malachi had predicted that the Messiah, 'the Lord whom you seek, will suddenly come to his temple' (Malachi 3: 1). The Temple was at the heart of Judaism. Jesus' action shows God's judgement on Israel: the house of God had been turned into a den of thieves:

- Animals for sacrifice had to be perfect, so traders were selling them for a big profit.
- Every male Jew had to pay a tax for the Temple's upkeep. This had to be paid with the special Temple coinage. Business was good for the moneychangers, who were probably making a lot of money.
- People were using the Temple, the holiest place in the world, as a

short-cut.

All this was happening in the Court of the Gentiles, the only part of the Temple into which the Gentiles could go. It was a 'house of prayer for all nations' (the Gentiles), not a market or a thoroughfare! Jesus enrages the Jewish authorities, who want him dead.

The question about authority
Read Mark 11.27-33

Jesus' questioners are identified as the chief priests, the teachers of the Law (scribes) and the elders.

Where does Jesus' authority come from? How can a carpenter interfere with the running of the Temple? The question is a trap. If Jesus says he gets his authority from God, he could be arrested for blasphemy. If he says he behaves in a way he thinks is right, he would lose face: only a maniac would make a claim like that.

Jesus brilliantly side-steps the question, and sets one of his own. Now the authorities cannot win. If they say John's authority came from God, Jesus will ask them why they did not believe him. After all, John pointed to Jesus. If they deny that John's authority came from God, they risk a riot. Everyone thinks John was a prophet. They cannot answer Jesus, and Jesus will not answer them.

The allegory of the vineyard
Read Mark 12.1-12

An allegory is a type of parable in which each event or person stands for something in reality.

Foreigners often bought land in Galilee and rented it to the locals; the locals resented it. This is the background to the story.

The allegory can be explained as follows:

- The vineyard owner is God.
- The vineyard is Israel. (In the Old Testament, Isaiah uses a vineyard as a symbol for Israel.)
- The tenants are the Jewish leaders, who behave badly.
- The slaves/servants are the prophets. God wants right action and

right religion from his people; the vineyard owner wants his share of the harvest. Both send messengers.

- The servants are beaten up or killed. The prophets were treated the same way.
- The vineyard owner decided to send his 'beloved son'. If the tenants do not listen to the messengers, they may listen to the son. The 'beloved son' of God is Jesus. (The voice from heaven calls him exactly that at his baptism and at the Transfiguration.)
- The tenants kill the man's son. The authorities will kill Jesus.
- The owner of the vineyard will kill the tenants. God will not allow the authorities to get away with Jesus' death, although how they will be punished is not stated.
- The owner will hand the vineyard over to others. The 'others' are the Gentiles, outcasts and sinners. They are now God's people, incorporated into his Kingdom. Israel is no longer the people of God.
- Just as some builders reject a piece of stone as useless, the authorities reject Jesus as the Messiah. Yet the stone will turn out to be the most important of all. Jesus will be shown to be the Messiah.

Again, the authorities are furious, but cannot act because of the crowd.

The question about paying taxes
Read Mark 12.13-17

This time it is the Pharisees and the Herodians who try to trap Jesus. We know very little about the Herodians: presumably they were members of Herod's party, the supporters of Herod Antipas.

The Jews hated paying Roman taxes. If Jesus tells them not to pay the tax, he will be popular with them. Yet the Romans could arrest him as a traitor. If he says they should pay the tax, people will stop following him. No Messiah would say that!

Jesus again gives a brilliant reply. The coin showed Caesar's head: it was legally his property. 'Render [give] to Caesar the things that are Caesar's, and to God the things that are God's.'

Some Christians have taken this to mean that Christians should always obey the government, though this is not what Jesus actually says. Others think he is implying that doing what God wants is more important than doing what human beings want. If there is a clash, Christians should obey God, not human authority.

The question about the resurrection of the dead
Read Mark 12.18-27

The **Sadducees**, who asked this question, were a small, aristocratic group. Many of them were wealthy, and they did not want trouble with the Romans which might affect their power. Many were priests in the Temple. They accepted only those ideas which were in the Torah, so they did not believe in angels or the Messiah. Nor did they believe in life after death (= 'the resurrection', which should not be confused with the resurrection of Jesus).

Their question here is designed to make belief in the resurrection look silly. It is based on a law in Deuteronomy. This says that if a married man has no children and dies, his brother must marry the widow so that the dead man's family line will continue. So, they ask, what happens if there are seven brothers, and none of them have children? If there is life after death ('the resurrection'), whose wife will she be?

Jesus does not go into detail, but he makes it clear that the dead will rise to life, and says that there will then be no marriage, as people will be 'like angels', though it is not clear what this means. As the Sadducees only accept the Torah, this is what Jesus quotes from. In Exodus, God spoke to Moses from a burning bush. God said, 'I am' (not 'I was') 'the God of Abraham, the God of Isaac, and the God of Jacob.' Abraham, Isaac and Jacob were long dead, but God's words imply that somehow they are still alive.

Christians believe in **life after death**. The New Testament seems to have two main ideas about it, as do Christians today:
1. After death, people go straight to heaven or hell: into God's presence, or totally separated from him. (The Roman Catholic Church's official line is that only very few people are good enough to go straight to heaven. Others first go to a 'place' called purgatory. Many Roman Catholics think of purgatory not so much as a place, but

as the pain of being separated from worldly things.

2. When people die, they will have to 'wait', to 'rest in peace', until God ends the universe (although it is difficult to know how time can have any meaning after death, so these two ideas may not be so different after all). Then the dead will rise and be judged. God will make a 'new heaven and a new earth' (Revelation 21.1). The New Testament is clear that people will have some sort of a body after death; they will not just be souls.

Christianity teaches that it is enough to trust in God and in his promises. God is too good and loving to let his friends be destroyed in death. However, he does not provide people with information about the furniture of heaven or the temperature of hell.

The greatest commandment
Read Mark 12.28-34

The teacher of the Law (scribe) is not trying to trap Jesus. He is genuinely interested in Jesus' answer to a favourite problem of the Rabbis. Which of the commandments in the Torah sums up all the others?

The command to 'love God' is from the beginning of the prayer called the Shema, from Deuteronomy 6.4-5. In Jesus' time, it was recited three times a day. It was written out and placed in boxes (phylacteries) strapped to the head and wrist during prayer times. Similar boxes were placed on the doorposts of Jewish homes. Both practices continue among Orthodox Jews today.

The command to 'love your neighbour as you love yourself' is from Leviticus 19.18. 'Neighbour' had been taken to mean 'fellow Israelite': here, it means 'everybody'.

Jesus was the first Jewish teacher to sum up the Torah with these two commandments.

As the scribe agrees with Jesus, he is not far from the Kingdom of God.

Mark's readers may have found this story useful in the debate over whether Gentile Christians have to keep the Torah. If they loved God and loved their neighbours, presumably the rest of the Torah was not necessary.

The question about the Messiah
Read Mark 12.35-37

Jesus now asks a question. David, who was believed to have written the psalms, calls the Christ 'My Lord'. So how can the scribes say the Christ is the Son of David? Surely he is *more* than that?

Some scholars have suggested that Jesus was not in fact descended from David. If this is right, stories like this one try to get round the problem. (The Jews believed the Messiah had to be descended from David, but Jesus was not.)

However, the New Testament is clear that Jesus *was* descended from David. If this is correct, Jesus is saying here that the Christ is more than the Son of David. (He certainly is not going to be a warrior at the head of a Jewish empire, as David was.)

Jesus warns against the teachers of the Law (scribes)
Read Mark 12.38-40

Jesus warns the crowd against the teachers of the Law:
1. They like walking around in long shawls (talliths), which were usually worn for prayer. They either have extra-large versions, or wear them all the time, or have extra large tassels on them. The point is that they like to be noticed. (The Greek here can also mean that they like to walk up and down in the Temple's covered walkways or 'porticoes'.)
2. They want people's respect but do not deserve it.
3. They want the best seats in the synagogue and at dinner parties.
4. They make a big to-do about praying, but extort money from needy people. Such behaviour can only earn them the greatest condemnation.

Revision tip:

Look back over the set texts from Mark 12.

Mark chapter 13

Mark 13 is rarely set for examinations and you may well be able to skip this section.

Read chapter 13 of Mark

Both the Jews and the early Christians believed that a day would come when God would wind up history. On that day, the good would be rewarded and the wicked punished.

Apocalyptic books were written about what would happen. ('Apocalyptic' comes from a Greek word meaning 'to uncover/reveal secrets'.) Examples of such books from the Bible include Daniel and Revelation. Chapter 13 of Mark claims to give Jesus' teaching about the end of the world. It is often called 'the Little Apocalypse', although its language and ideas are not as extreme or strange as other apocalyptic books.

How much of it goes back to Jesus himself is debated by scholars.

It is addressed to Peter, James and John, the inner group of the disciples.

The passage's teaching about the end is as follows:

- The Temple will be destroyed. (The Romans did destroy it in AD 70.)
- People will come and claim falsely to speak for Jesus, saying 'I am he!'
- There will be wars, rumours of wars, earthquakes and famines. The Christians must not get too excited: these are not signs that the end will be very soon.
- They are like the first pangs of childbirth: they show that something is going to happen, but not the precise time.
- Christians will suffer for their faith
  - before a court;
  - before rulers and kings;
  - by being put to death by members of their own family;
  - by being hated by everyone.
- But there are promises, too:
  - The Holy Spirit will speak for the Christians when they are in court. God will guide them in what to say.
  - Whoever holds out to the end will be saved. This may fit in with the situation in Mark's Church, which may have been persecuted by Nero. Christians have been persecuted for their faith throughout history.
- The gospel must be preached to all nations (Gentiles) before the end will come. This idea has inspired many missionaries.
- When the 'abomination of desolation' ('the awful horror' in the Good News Bible's translation) is set up, people in Judea must flee to the hills. Escape will be hard for pregnant women and for those with young children, and harder still in winter.
- The verses about running away to the mountains seem to be talking about fleeing from a siege. The Romans besieged Jerusalem in AD 70. The events of this siege

58

may be what the 'abomination of desolation' means.

- Others have suggested the abomination refers to the coming of the Antichrist (the devil or his representative) at the end of the world. Or it could refer to the attempt made by the Emperor Caligula to set up his statue in the Temple in AD 40.
- God has shortened the days of suffering before the end. This is because of his concern for his chosen people.
- Imposters claiming to be prophets or even to be Jesus will try to dazzle people and lead them astray. Even if they perform miracles, the Christians should not believe them.
- The final and full arrival of the Kingdom of God will be when Jesus returns. The idea of the Son of Man coming on clouds is best understood as picture language.
- When a fig tree puts out its leaves, it shows that summer is near. When the disciples see these things happening, they should realize that the end is near. The events will take place before all those now living have died. Mark 13 now seems, after all, to be saying that the end will be soon. Perhaps a different source is being used here.
- Jesus' words will never pass away.
- No one, not even Jesus, knows exactly when the end will come. Only God the Father knows. The Christians should not try to work out a timetable for the end. The 'servants' (Christians) do not know when their master will come back. So they must keep awake and be ready for him.

Son of Man

Questions on 'Son of Man' on the exam paper are fairly popular. This topic needs to be learnt thoroughly; lots of candidates do not understand what it means.

People will say that 'Son of Man' shows Jesus was a human being (as well as God). **They're wrong. This is not what it means.**

It's also said that 'Son of Man' is a title of Jesus. In fact, it's not clear whether it's a title at all.

For the exam, it's not necessary to learn all the debate about the meaning of the term (or title). However, it *is* worth knowing that the expression 'son of man' was used in two ways by Jewish people:

1. **'son of man' just meant any human being**. It was an expression meaning 'this man here' or just 'someone'.

BUT

2. **THE** Son of Man was a figure who appeared in some Jewish apocalyptic books. He was a heavenly being who performed miracles and would judge human beings.

This Son of Man may have been the same as the Messiah, or he may not. He was the same sort of thing, though – even if he was more 'supernatural' than the new, Greater King David.

The problem is that the kind of Son of Man in number 2 may reflect an idea held by some Jews long *after* Jesus' time and not before it. (See p. 58 for the meaning of 'apocalyptic'.) So it may not have influenced Jesus at all.

So:
- It's best not to say that the Son of Man and the Messiah mean the same thing.
- There's a strong case for saying that, when Jesus called himself 'the Son of Man', he was just saying 'this man here'. In other words, 'me' or 'I'. (So, 'the Son of Man has authority on earth to forgive sins' could be translated 'This man here has authority on earth to forgive sins'.) Jesus preferred to say 'son of man' = 'this man here' because it wasn't 'loaded', as the title 'Messiah' was.

It's important to state
- **Only Jesus uses the words 'son of man'** in Mark. No-one else does.
- In Mark, there are **three** ideas Jesus conveys about the Son of Man:
  1. the Son of Man has **authority on earth**;
  2. the Son of Man must **suffer, die and rise again**
  3. the Son of Man will **return at the end of time**

In a bit more detail, then:

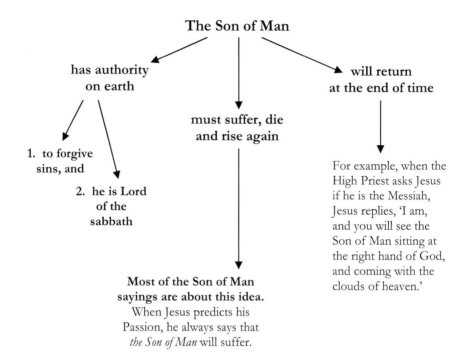

The Son of Man

has authority on earth

1. to forgive sins, and
2. he is Lord of the sabbath

must suffer, die and rise again

Most of the Son of Man sayings are about this idea. When Jesus predicts his Passion, he always says that *the Son of Man* will suffer.

will return at the end of time

For example, when the High Priest asks Jesus if he is the Messiah, Jesus replies, 'I am, and you will see the Son of Man sitting at the right hand of God, and coming with the clouds of heaven.'

If you're asked what 'Son of Man' means for Christians today, a reasonable answer is to say that it gets across the three ideas above: that Jesus has authority, that he suffers and rises, and that he will return. You can comment that this is also the way it is used in Mark. While the title (if it is a title!) *isn't* linked to the doctrine that Jesus was fully human, you could say something like ' "Son of Man" could be said to emphasise Jesus' humanity, because the phrase could just mean "a human being" to Jews in Jesus' time.'

Mark chapter 14

The plot against Jesus
Read Mark 14.1-2

Passover recalled how God rescued the Jews from the Egyptians. He appointed Moses as their leader, and brought them through the Red Sea to the promised land of Israel.

The Festival of Unleavened Bread lasted for seven days after the Passover; it marked the beginning of the barley harvest. Its name also reminded the people that, when God brought them out of Egypt, there was not even time to wait for their bread to rise.

Every good Jew wanted to spend at least one Passover in Jerusalem. The city was crammed with pilgrims. Patriotic feelings ran high. People with Zealot sympathies might be hoping that God would save them from the Romans, just as he had saved them from the Egyptians. So the chief priests and scribes are afraid of a riot, even though they still want Jesus arrested.

From now on, the story runs without a break. Mark spends a great deal of time on the Passion, which shows it was important to him and to his readers. **Why was Jesus' death so important to the early Christians?**

Jesus died at Passover time. The Passover was seen as the foundation of the **covenant** or agreement between God and his people. The Jews agreed to keep the Torah and God agreed to be their special God. They kept God's covenant by worshipping him. Sacrifice in the Temple was an important part of this worship and it was believed many sacrifices could *take away sin*.

The Christians came to realize that **Jesus' death was *like* a sacrifice**. But it was a perfect sacrifice. It did not take away only some sins of the Jews: it took away the sins of the whole world. God once saved his people from Egypt and gave them a covenant. Now, he had raised Jesus from the dead, and had therefore saved everyone from death itself. He was offering everyone a new relationship with him: a **new covenant.**

Christians today still believe this. No matter how hard people try, they will never be as good as they ought to be. If the world were judged in a sort of cosmic law court, no one would do very well. Yet God did not want that to happen. The love and obedience Jesus had in dying can somehow make up for everything human beings do wrong. It puts everything right between people and God, and is therefore called the **atonement** (at-one-ment).

Christians believe that people need to receive the benefits of the atonement. Protestant Christians believe that people only need faith to enable them to share in Jesus' saving work. Catholic Christians emphasize more than Protestants the need for 'good works': loving

God and our neighbours.

It is clear what the atonement *is*, but not precisely how it works. People use different models – picture language – to help them understand it. The idea of Jesus' death as a sacrifice is one model. There are other models, too:

- If you were unable to offer a sacrifice to show you were sorry for wrongdoing, you could pay money instead. Jesus' death acts like this payment, and it is Jesus who pays it on everyone's behalf.
- People are slaves to sin. Jesus' death releases or 'redeems' them from their slavery.
- People owe God a 'fine' as punishment for their sin. Jesus' death pays the fine.
- In Jesus' death, God enters into the suffering of the world. By his resurrection, Jesus offers people a way through that suffering.

It is important to remember that these are models. Their picture language helps us to understand the atonement, but they all fall short of a complete picture.

Jesus' anointing
Read Mark 14.3-9

Jesus mixes with outcasts right to the end. Here, he is in the house of Simon the leper. Lepers were ceremonially unclean: barred from worship or contact with God's people.

It was polite to pour a little perfume on guests who arrived at your house. Yet the woman is not Jesus' host, and she uses a whole jar of very expensive perfume, showing how important Jesus is to her.

The meaning of this action is twofold:
1. When people died, their bodies were anointed with perfume. The jars were not reused: they were broken, and the pieces were placed in the tomb. The woman anoints Jesus for burial.
2. 'Christ' and 'Messiah' both mean 'the anointed one'. It is now that the Christ is anointed. Yet it is not Elijah who does so: it is a woman. Women were considered to be second-class citizens in Jesus' day, yet a woman is here given the highest honour. And Jesus is anointed as Messiah when he is about to suffer and die.

Jesus rebukes the other guests. Being good to the poor is important, but it does not rule out other generous actions.

Judas
Read Mark 14.10-11

Judas' offer enables the chief priests to arrest Jesus quietly, without fear of a riot.

It may be that Judas betrayed Jesus because he was a Zealot and was disappointed when Jesus did not turn out to be the sort of Messiah he wanted. Or he may have done it for the money.

The Last Supper
Read Mark 14.12-31

Jesus' instructions to the disciples about finding a room show that he is in control of what was happening. It is not clear whether Jesus has arranged in advance with the man carrying the water jar, or whether Mark thinks it is a miracle. (It may have been arranged in advance: women usually carried water jars. A man carrying one looks like a pre-arranged signal.)

Mark believes that the Last Supper was a Passover meal. This was – and still is – the meal eaten by Jews to remember the events of the first Passover, when God rescued his people from Egypt. The Angel of Death passed over the Jewish homes, whose doors were daubed with the blood of the Passover lambs, but he killed the firstborn sons of the Egyptians. In Jesus' day, the lamb for each family's meal was taken to the Temple to be slaughtered by the priests as a sacrifice, and then taken home to be cooked and eaten.

Jesus' words in verse 21 show that the whole of the Passion fulfils the Old Testament. This includes Judas' betrayal. Compare Mark's account with Psalm 41.9:

> Even my bosom friend in whom I trusted,
> who ate of my bread, has lifted his heel against me.

It would have been better for Judas if he had not been born. This may mean he will go to hell, or it may refer to his death. Matthew's

Gospel says that Judas was so stricken with guilt that he hanged himself. Jesus may mean it would have been better not to have been born than to suffer this.

Jesus' words and actions over the bread and wine have always stood at the heart of Christian worship.

Jesus acts as any Jewish host in taking the bread, thanking God for it, and breaking it. Yet he adds that the bread is his body. Just as the bread is broken at the Passover meal, Jesus' body will be broken on the cross.

The wine at the Passover meal symbolized the agreement or covenant between God and the Jews. Jesus takes the cup, and again thanks God. Yet he adds the extraordinary words:

> This is my blood of the new covenant, which is poured out for many.

> (The word 'new' is only in some Greek manuscripts.
> Whether it's original or not, it still conveys the meaning.)

In the Old Testament, the prophet Jeremiah predicted that God would make a new covenant with the people, and he would forgive their sins. Jesus makes the new covenant here.

- The old covenant was sealed by the blood of sacrifices, especially that of the Passover lamb.
- The new covenant is sealed by the blood of Jesus, who is sacrificed on the cross.

When Moses sealed the first covenant, he threw the blood on the people, saying, 'Behold the blood of the covenant which the LORD has made with you' (Exodus 24.8). When the Jews ate the Passover lamb and were sprinkled with the blood of Moses' sacrifice, they became and remained the people of God's first covenant. Now the old sacrifices are replaced by Jesus' death. When people eat and drink at the Eucharist, they are part of God's new covenant.

Jesus will not drink wine again until he drinks the new wine of the Messianic Banquet, the Kingdom of God. So the Last Supper and the Eucharist, which re-enacts it, are a foretaste of what is to come: the fellowship with Christ in heaven.

Jesus further predicts that all the disciples will fall away, as predicted in the OT (he quotes from Zechariah 13.7). The disciples say that they will stay faithful, yet Peter is told that he will deny Jesus three times before the cock has crowed twice. The next time they will see him is after the resurrection, 'in Galilee'.

Jesus in Gethsemane
Read Mark 14.32-52

There area number of things to note about this passage:

- Gethsemane was an olive grove on the Mount of Olives.
- Jesus is genuinely terrified by death, although he has the courage to drink the 'cup' that is offered to him.
- Jesus calls God 'Abba' in prayer. This is the Aramaic word for 'Dad' or 'Daddy'. Jews did not use it because it was too informal. The early Christians did use it in their worship.
- The gang of men whom Judas brings are from the Sanhedrin, the Jewish council.
- Jesus is not an 'outlaw' or Zealot. He stops the scuffle.
- The disciples run off. They do not meet Jesus again until after he is raised from the dead.
- The young man who runs away naked is a curious detail. It has been suggested that he is an eyewitness from whom Mark got his information, or even that he is Mark himself.
- The events of this night from the Last Supper onwards are remembered by Christians on Maundy Thursday, the Thursday of Holy Week. (In the Roman Catholic Church, it's more usually called Holy Thursday.) At the Maundy Thursday Eucharist, the readings recall the night's events. There is often a vigil afterwards, which is usually held in one of the side chapels. People will pray through the night, remembering Jesus' agony in the garden as though they are watching with him.

Jesus' trial before the Sanhedrin
Read Mark 14.53-65

Mark presents the Sanhedrin as breaking every rule in the book in their determination to have Jesus put to death:

- The witnesses lie. They claim Jesus spoke against the Temple, saying he would destroy it. (Jesus had in fact predicted its destruction, but had not said that he would do it.) The charge is dropped because they cannot agree.

- The high priest, Caiaphas, tries a direct question. It is likely that this was breaking the Sanhedrin's own rules. He asks Jesus point blank whether he is the Messiah.

Jesus' reply to the high priest's question shows:
- **The Messianic Secret is over.** As he is now in the middle of his Passion, he is in truth the Messiah, because the Messiah's job is to suffer, die and rise again.
- Jesus will be exalted to the place of honour with God the Father: he will sit at his right hand. (This is picture language, not to be taken literally.) And he will return. It looks at first as though this will happen soon, because the high priest will 'see' it. But it may mean that he will 'see' or 'realise' that Jesus is at God's right hand: that he is the Son of Man, who will eventually return on the clouds of heaven.

The high priest ceremonially tears his robes, which was a sign that he had heard blasphemy. As the Romans did not allow the council to execute prisoners, he is to be handed over to the governor. Some of them actually assault Jesus, underlining the injustice of the trial and emphasizing that Jesus suffered.

Peter denies Jesus
Read Mark 14.66-72

This story must originally have come from Peter. Peter denies Jesus at the same moment as Jesus admits that he is the Messiah. Yet Peter will be forgiven by Jesus (see Mark 16.7).

Mark chapter 15

Jesus before Pilate
Read Mark 15.1-20

The members of the Sanhedrin meet again in the morning and confirm their plans.

Pontius Pilate was the Roman governor ('procurator' or 'prefect') of Judea. According to the Jewish historian Josephus, he was a cruel and stubborn man.

Jesus is condemned as the Messiah. This is translated as 'king of the Jews' for Pilate's benefit: the crime is treason against Rome. Yet although Jesus is not a political Messiah, it is as the Messiah that he is put to death.

Jesus' reply to Pilate's question ('So you say') means something like, 'That's how you put it, not how I put it.'

The tradition of Passover amnesty, the release of a prisoner during the festival, is only mentioned by the Gospels. It is odd that Pilate is presented as having to release either Barabbas or Jesus: why could he not release both?

However, it shows that Mark does not think Pilate is really guilty of Jesus' death. The blame lies far more with the people, especially the Jewish authorities. It is important to remember that Christianity spread very quickly through the Roman world. It was bound to attract the attention of the Imperial authorities. They might well not take too kindly to it if they knew its founder had been executed by a Roman judge as a traitor against Rome. So the Gospel writers emphasize that Pilate's hand was forced. He did not really want to execute Jesus.

The crowd chooses a murderer in preference to their Messiah, and Jesus is savagely beaten by being scourged or whipped. The soldiers make fun of his claim to be a king: again, Jesus' suffering is emphasized. He really is a king, even though the soldiers ridicule his claim.

The crucifixion
Read Mark 15.21-41

Crucifixion was a form of execution often used by the Romans. It was a savage punishment, designed to cause the maximum suffering and therefore serve as a strong deterrent to others.

The following points about this passage need to be noted:

- Simon of Cyrene helps Jesus to carry the horizontal beam of his cross. Jesus has been beaten too badly to carry it himself. Simon's sons are mentioned, which may show he is an eyewitness, and that his sons are known to Mark's Church.
- Golgotha is Aramaic for 'place of the skull'. We are not now certain of the site.
- Jesus refuses the offer of a painkiller (wine mixed with myrrh).
- The execution squad was entitled to a condemned man's clothes, so they dice for them.
- The notice above the cross gave the criminal's offence. Pilate may have meant it to frighten other would-be Messiahs, or as an insult to the Jewish authorities. It underlines, again, that Jesus is executed as the Messiah.
- The fact that Jesus is executed with two bandits shows him in the company of outcasts, even at his death.
- The jeering of the passers-by, and of the chief priests and scribes, misses the point. The Messiah must stay on the cross, not come down from it. This is what his work means.
- The darkness from noon until 3 p.m. may have been a sandstorm or a thunderstorm, or Mark may think it is a supernatural darkness. The Old Testament prophet Amos had predicted that God would 'make the sun go down at noon' (Amos 8.9). The darkness shows God is at work.
- 'Eloi, Eloi, lama sabachthani?' is translated: 'My God, my God, why have you abandoned me?' This is a quotation of the first line of Psalm 22. The psalm ends with God saving the person who is suffering. It has been suggested that Jesus has this in mind: God will show him to be in the right, too. However, it is more likely that it underlines the intensity of Jesus' suffering. Even he feels he has been abandoned by God.
- People mistake Eloi for 'Elijah', and think he is waiting for the prophet's help. The offer of wine is probably meant as a sick, half-joking experiment.

- When Jesus dies, the Temple curtain is ripped in two. This separated the Holy of Holies, the most sacred part of the Temple, from the rest of the building. This detail may mean one of three things:
    - The Temple will be destroyed (as it was in AD 70 by Rome).
    - The barrier of sin which separates God and human beings has been destroyed by Jesus' death.
    - The Temple is no longer the place to find God: God is now to be found in Jesus.
- The centurion confesses Jesus to be the Son of God. It is a Gentile, not a Jew, who makes this statement, and he makes it at the moment of Jesus' death. It is the man on the cross who is most truly the Son of God.
- Some women who had followed Jesus when he was in Galilee watched what happened. Their faithfulness contrasts with the way the male disciples ran away in terror.

Jesus' burial
Read Mark 15.42-47

A member of the Sanhedrin, Joseph of Arimathea, asks Pilate for Jesus' body and buries it. Jewish burial customs were strict, and the Romans seem to have respected them here: bodies had to be buried on the day of death, if possible. It was made more urgent by the fact that the next day was the Sabbath. The body could not be buried then: that would count as work. The tomb is carefully sealed.

Christians remember the death and burial of Jesus on Good Friday, the Friday of Holy Week.

Mark chapter 16

The resurrection
Mark 16.1-8

The original text of Mark records the fact of the resurrection, but does *not* mention any appearances of the risen Jesus to his disciples.

The women go to anoint Jesus' body, which Joseph has not had time to do. The 'young man' is probably meant to be an angel. Jesus is not in the tomb but has been raised to life. The women are to tell the disciples that Jesus is going before them to Galilee, where they will see him. By singling out Peter for special mention, Mark is probably indicating that Jesus will forgive him.

The women are terrified. This is the sort of fear that the disciples felt when Jesus calmed the storm, and which made the Jews tremble when God gave Moses the Ten Commandments. It is the fear of God: the way people react when God is at work.

And this is where Mark's Gospel ends. No appearances of the risen Jesus. No moving, final meeting between Peter and Christ. Just a few terrified women, too frightened to speak, running away from Jesus' tomb.

It seems pretty abrupt.

A couple of writers in the second century thought so too. After all, Matthew, Luke and John all go on to tell stories about Jesus' appearances to his disciples in Galilee and Jerusalem. So these second century writers each had a go – not very successfully – at finishing Mark's Gospel off for him. (Their attempts are printed in Bibles as Mark 16.9-20.)

But here, Mark ends. Perhaps he meant to carry on; some scholars think he did. Maybe the ending was lost. Most New Testament experts today, though, think Mark knew exactly what he was doing by stopping at this point. As he was the first Gospel writer, why shouldn't he end where he liked? And ending on a cliffhanger, at the most important point, is a good way to finish the book. After all, the message is out:

Jesus is risen.

(Some examination boards require candidates to know about the debate as to whether Mark *intended* to finish his work here. There is a section on this on pp. 74-75.)

The meaning of the resurrection

The resurrection has always been at the heart of Christianity. It was and is vitally important:

- It showed that God approved of Jesus.
- It showed that Jesus was who he said he was, and that what he said was true.
- It was God's new saving act. The crucifixion makes no sense without the resurrection. Jesus took away the sins of the world on the cross, and offers people a new life by his resurrection.
- It shows that death is not the end. God raised Jesus to life, and he will raise his people to life as well.

But is it true?

The earliest Christians certainly thought it was. Many of the first disciples died for their faith in Jesus. It is almost impossible to see why they would have died for something they had made up. They were convinced that they had met the risen Jesus. In his first letter to the church at Corinth, Paul says that many of the original eyewitnesses were still alive when he was writing (in AD54/55). He also makes the extraordinary statement that he, too, had seen the risen Jesus. Even non-Christian scholars of the New Testament agree that the disciples genuinely believed that they had experienced the risen Jesus.

It is therefore very difficult to believe that the disciples stole the body or fantasized the whole thing. It is psychologically ridiculous. Neither is it easy to believe that Jesus survived crucifixion and pretended he was risen. That is physically impossible. Furthermore, it makes Jesus a fraud and a liar and the disciples unrealistically stupid. The idea that the disciples hallucinated assumes that they all did so, but hallucinations are seen by individuals, not by groups. And figures in a hallucination do not behave in the way the risen Jesus is said to have behaved. If the Jewish or Roman authorities stole the body, why did they not produce it to kill off the new religion which caused them so much trouble?

Of course, if there is no God, then Jesus remains dead and buried. Yet there are good reasons to believe that there is a God. And these are intelligent, philosophical reasons: they are far more than cultural conditioning. If Jesus was right about God, would not God act in the way that Christians say he did, by raising Jesus from the dead?

The longer ending, added to Mark
Read Mark 16.9-20

This section of the Gospel is part of the Bible, even though Mark is not the writer. As the exam boards tend to set Mark rather than the other Gospels, it's natural that they'd want to set what the (addition to) Mark's Gospel says about the resurrection.

It is very important to remember, though:

1. **Mark did not write this section.** It was added later, well into the second century, by another – and very much less sophisticated – writer. The best Greek manuscripts of Mark leave it out altogether.

2. Christians who realise this was added to Mark – and many of them don't, as they're not biblical scholars – don't give it the same status or authority as the rest of Mark's text. They would accord much more authority to the accounts of the appearances of the risen Jesus in the other Gospels.

3. So, while it's interesting as part of the history of Christianity, it's not at all reliable as an account of the resurrection of Jesus (except where it's backed up, as it is in a few details, by the other Gospels – but most of it is not). Much of it seems to come from the lunatic fringes of early Christianity: the promises that Christians can handle deadly snakes, drink poison and so on, plus the promise of hellfire for those who are not baptised, are not the words of the risen Jesus. They are far too silly (and nasty, too).

The writer, whose name in fact may have been Ariston, gives several appearances of the risen Jesus:

- Jesus appears to **Mary Magdalene**. Her companions do not believe her when she tells them about it.

- Jesus appears to **two of them** while they were walking in the country. Again, the others do not believe it.

- Jesus appears to **the eleven disciples** while they are at table. They are told to preach the gospel. Those who are baptized and who believe will be saved; the rest will be condemned. Believers will be able to perform bizarre miracles.

Jesus is taken up into heaven. The disciples preached the gospel, which the Lord confirmed by the miracles that accompanied it. The ascension of Jesus need not be taken literally; some would say it is a symbolic way of marking the end of the resurrection appearances.

Revision tip:

Mark 14-16 are key chapters and the exam often tests knowledge of them. Make sure you know them very thoroughly.
Read the text again or listen to it on the CD and test yourself with the questions at the back of this book.
Keep doing this until you've learnt it.
Again, it's best to do this with breaks between the learning sessions – an hour, a day or even a few days – rather than trying to cram it all in at once.

Did Mark intend to finish his Gospel at 16.8?

The table below gives the main arguments. Not all exam boards set this topic and you may be able to skip over this section.

Mark *did not* intend to finish at 16.8	Mark *did* intend to finish at 16.8
Mark calls his book a 'gospel': good news. We'd expect him to end with better news than the women running off!	But the message that Jesus is risen *is* good news. The whole Gospel has been leading to this moment.
Mark says the women 'said nothing to anyone'. But we'd expect him to say the story would come out. Matthew, Luke and John have accounts of the risen Jesus appearing to the disciples; we'd expect Mark to, too.	Mark may not mean that the women *never* said anything. The tone of Mark's Gospel concentrates more on Jesus' suffering than on his glory; maybe this is why he omits the resurrection appearances. Perhaps, too, his readers knew the appearance stories very well anyway.
Jesus predicts his resurrection and the young man says to the women that they will see him in Galilee. Why doesn't he record how this came true?	Why should he? Isn't the promise enough on its own?

Mark *did not* intend to finish at 16.8	Mark *did* intend to finish at 16.8
The last word in 16.8 in Greek is 'gar', which means 'because' or 'for'. Ending a Greek sentence with 'gar' is as odd as ending an English sentence with 'because'.	No it isn't. 'Gar' ends other books in Greek. In any case, Mark's Greek was not great and he makes lots of stylistic errors, so it may be inelegant, but then that's the way he writes.
Mark intended to write more but either the ending he actually wrote was lost, or something else happened. Books in Mark's time were written on scrolls or sheets of papyrus, which tore easily. The verses after 'gar' in 16.8 could have been torn off accidentally or damaged in some way. Or Mark may have died or been arrested at that point.	It's not very likely, is it? It's even more unlikely because he stops at a place where it looks as though he could have *meant* to stop. In any case, we now know that it *was* common then to write in the sort of book that we use today, like the one you're holding now: sheets of paper bound at the spine. The technical name for this sort of book is a codex; Mark may well have written on a codex, not a scroll or separate pages. And surely there would have been lots of copies of Mark? Couldn't the lost ending have been reconstructed? It seems very, very unlikely that Mark was arrested by the Romans or had a heart attack while the ink on 16.8 was still wet.

Revision notes on Mark and Christianity today

This section gives notes on the following topics:

1. The authority of Mark's Gospel for Christians today
2. The Trinity and beliefs about Jesus
3. Baptism
4. The Eucharist / the Mass
5. Persecution and Christianity today
6. Mark and community cohesion

Not all boards set all of these topics. Once again, check your exam board's specification or ask your RS teacher which of them you need to learn, and ignore the others.

The authority of Mark's Gospel for Christians today

The Bible has *authority* for Christians. Mark's Gospel is part of the Bible, and therefore Mark has authority for Christians.

But different Christians have different ideas about how accurate the Bible is, and how much of it should be followed in daily life. Some say it is 100% accurate and that its teaching must always be obeyed. Others think it is not as simple as that.

Revision tip

Exam boards expect candidates to be able to show they are aware of differences within Christianity.
So it's important to show you're awareness, if you're asked, of different Christian views about the authority of Mark.

We can put the different views about the authority of Mark on a diagram, which shows (and names) the possible opinions.

The spectrum of opinion:
How Christians today see the authority of Mark's Gospel

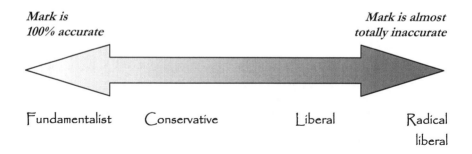

*Mark is
100% accurate*

*Mark is almost
totally inaccurate*

Fundamentalist   Conservative   Liberal   Radical
                                                                                                                      liberal

What the terms mean:

1. Fundamentalist

A **fundamentalist** (when talking about the Bible) believes:

- Everything in the Bible is 100% accurate.
- God the Holy Spirit stopped the writers of the Bible from making any errors whatsoever.
- If there appear to be errors in the Bible, another explanation needs to be found. If the Bible disagrees with modern science, then science must be wrong. If the Bible appears to contradict itself, then we must look for a different explanation of how the different bits fit together.
- Everything is Mark's Gospel is absolutely true. Mark wrote things down exactly as they happened. God stopped him from making even a single mistake.
- Many fundamentalists also say the Bible always describes literally how things happened. (So there are no myths or legends in the Bible; it all just happened.) We can call these fundamentalists 'literalists'.

2. Conservative

A **conservative** here doesn't mean someone who votes Tory. The word here is applied to the way people see the Bible.

Conservatives do not go as far as fundamentalists. Conservatives would be very unhappy with the idea that Mark makes enormous errors. They would certainly be very unhappy with the idea that Mark has basically got the whole thing wrong. They would say, in fact, that Mark is normally right.

After all, they might point to the idea that Mark knew Peter. Peter knew Jesus. So Mark had access to a completely accurate, eyewitness source.

Conservatives, then, would be willing to admit that Mark may just occasionally be inaccurate, or that he does not necessarily always record events in the order in which they happened. Like fundamentalists, they might say that the Holy Spirit stopped the material about Jesus from veering too far from the truth. After all, why would God bother to become human as Jesus, to die to save people from death, only to have the historical record about him be totally distorted by sloppy transmission of material?

Conservatives would say that Mark can be trusted. What he says should be followed as an accurate record of Jesus' life and teaching.

3. Liberal

Again, nothing to do with politics, but a way of looking at the Bible. Much of the research that has been done on the New Testament and on Mark is liberal, though by no means all of it.

Liberals note that the stories about Jesus were passed on by word of mouth before they were written down. The time when this happened is called the *oral period*; it lasted for about thirty years, from Jesus' crucifixion until Mark wrote his Gospel.

Liberals assume that the earliest Christians were not really interested in what happened. They were just interested in the message about their faith. The information about Jesus was not, they say, transmitted at all accurately during the oral period.

Liberals argue that, as the Gospels are first century documents, the writers of these documents had very simple ideas. They were also superstitious: they believed in things like demons, angels, miracles and so on. So they added this picture of the world onto the genuine information about Jesus. They didn't distinguish between reality and fable. If it worked for the message, fine.

Liberals would say we now know very little about what Jesus was *actually* like. The Gospels are written to persuade people to follow Christianity, not to record history.

Mark's Gospel is not important because it describes what happened. It's important because of the message that it contains. It doesn't matter that Mark gets so much so very wrong. And so the question, 'What does it mean?' is more important than the question, 'Did it happen?'

Radical liberals would say that we know so little about Jesus that Mark isn't really important at all. We must just try to live as God would want us, by being kind to other people.

Liberals range from people who think like this to those who would say, for example, that Mark does have a lot of accurate information. We can trust his overall picture of Jesus, even if we can't rely on every single detail. Perhaps Jesus did not do all the miracles, say, but his message about love for others is still important.

Looking deeper

There are some things we can add here.
- It's important to remember that Christians' attitude to the authority of the Bible form a *spectrum* of opinion. There is a range of ideas, not just three positions. So:
  - Not all conservatives agree with other conservatives.
  - Not all liberals agree with other liberals, or with radical liberals.
  - Some fundamentalists would say that only fundamentalists are really Christians.
- Most Christians are not fundamentalists, although most Christians are fairly conservative. Most Christians through history have been on the conservative end of things.
- It's not very easy to match 'conservative', 'fundamentalist' or 'liberal' to the different Churches. There are conservatives, liberals and fundamentalists in nearly all the main Christian denominations. There are liberal Anglicans, conservative Anglicans, fundamentalist Anglicans; liberal Methodists, conservative Methodists, fundamentalist Methodists... and so on. However, we can say:

- Biblical fundamentalists tend to be found in the Protestant Churches;
- Roman Catholics tend to be conservative but not fundamentalist;
- Liberals tend not to be Roman Catholics.

Some people find it hard to realise that the fundamentalist and conservative positions are not the only possible ones for Christians. Liberals are also Christians.

Liberalism is *not* just a view of the Bible held by scholars who are atheists (people who do not believe in God). Christianity allows the Bible to be studied. In fact, Christianity encourages it. After all, if the Bible is in some sense the Word of God, then it is absolutely vital to understand it properly. In the past, the Bible has been used to justify racism, sexism, wars of conquest and tyranny (none of which, of course, it *actually* supports).

St Augustine, an early Christian writer, suggested that any Christian interpretation of the Bible should build up both love of God and love of neighbour (this is based on the discussion Jesus had with the scribe in Mark 12.28-34).

Suppose we apply this to today. Parts of the Old Testament support the idea of a holy war. The Old Testament says God frequently wanted the Israelites to butcher their enemies, including the children (see Joshua 6.15-21, for example).

Would it really help people to love God or their neighbour if they had to believe, as a fundamentalist might say, that this really happened?

Or suppose we take the radical liberal view that Jesus is an obscure historical figure about whom we can know virtually nothing. Would that help people to love God?

The Trinity and beliefs about Jesus

It's important to remember that Christianity teaches that **Jesus was a human being.** He was fully human: as human as any other man, woman or child is human.

Yet Christianity teaches that **Jesus was also God.**

So, Christians believe that **God became a human being.**

The idea that God became a man as Jesus is called the Incarnation.

Christians, then, believe that **Jesus is fully human and fully God.**

Christians agree with other religions that there is one God, but Christians go on to say that God exists in three ways at once:

- God the Father
- God the Son
- God the Holy Spirit

The religious teaching (or **doctrine**) that God exists in three ways at once is called the doctrine of the **Trinity.** **'Trinity' means 'tri-unity': three-in-one.**

As God has no physical form, he is sometimes represented in Christian art by a triangle. This image helps us to understand more about the Trinity:

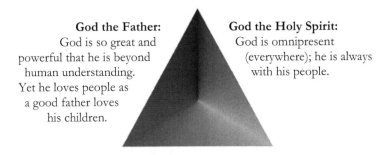

God the Father:
God is so great and powerful that he is beyond human understanding. Yet he loves people as a good father loves his children.

God the Holy Spirit:
God is omnipresent (everywhere); he is always with his people.

God the Son:
We would not know what God was like unless he showed us.
God became a human being as Jesus Christ.

- The three 'parts' of the Trinity are called the three **Persons** of the Trinity. 'Persons' does not means the same here as 'people' or 'individuals':
- **'Person' means 'aspect'.** Christians believe that God has three aspects; **God has three ways of being God.**
- All three Persons of the Trinity have always existed, and always will exist. They are **_eternal._**
- All three Persons of the Trinity are **equal.** Despite their names, the

Father is not greater than the Son or the Holy Spirit.

- All three Persons are usually called 'he'. This does not mean that God is male, but it does show that God has a personality. The Holy Spirit is 'he', not 'it'. (Some modern Christians are not happy with calling God 'he'. They agree that God is neither male nor female, but think calling God 'he' sounds sexist. We haven't the space to go into this debate fully. Christians have called God 'he' for two thousand years, and Jesus, in his own language, referred to God as 'he'.)

- **God the Son became a human being as Jesus. The Father and the Holy Spirit did not.** However, all three Persons of the Trinity work together – it was not as though the Father and the Holy Spirit did not know what the Son was up to!

- **All three Persons of the Trinity are *fully* God**, not one third of God. So, **as Jesus was God the Son made human, Jesus is *fully* God,** not one third of God.

Someone might ask, 'But how could God become a human being? They're too different.' After all:

God is everywhere (omnipresent); people are not;
God is all-powerful (omnipotent); people are not;
God is entirely good (omnibenevolent); people are not;
God knows everything (he is omniscient); people are not;
God is eternal: he always has existed and always will exist; people are conceived, are born, and die.

We could say that trying to fit God into a human being would be like trying to get a double-decker bus into a matchbox.

Clearly, then, if God is going to become a human being, he is going to have to give some things up. A human being cannot be everywhere, cannot be all-powerful, and does not know everything. To become human, God would have to give up being everywhere. He would have to give up most of his power and most or all of his knowledge.

Jesus was not God *disguised as* a human being. Nor was he a sort of puppet, with God pulling the strings all the time. Jesus was fully human and fully God.

So why did God bother?

Christianity teaches that God is so great that he is far beyond human understanding. Our minds cannot comprehend something that is infinite and has enough power to create the universe just by thinking it into existence.

But if God 'scaled himself down' to our size, we'd be able to understand him. We'd be able to get an accurate idea of him.

We may not be able to understand God, but we can understand a human being. So, God scales himself down. He becomes a human being. Christians believe he did this to show us what sort of a God he is – what he's like.

If someone asks, 'What's God like?', Christians would say they have the answer. God is 'like' Jesus. The sort of person Jesus was is the sort of person God is. Jesus was loving, generous, forgiving, understanding, kind; he was willing to welcome everyone into his friendship, no matter what they had done, or who they were. He paid no attention to the barriers human society put up of race, class or gender. The only people he condemned were those who thought they were perfect and didn't need help.

Christians also believe that God became a human being to save us from our sins. Jesus' execution on the cross abolished death.

To sum up, then, Christianity teaches:

Jesus *was* God, and because he rose from the dead, Jesus *still is* God.

God became a human being, and because Jesus rose from the dead, God still is a human being.

Jesus was – and is – fully God and fully human.

Revision tip:

This exercise will help you to revise this topic.
It's worth coming back to, as well.
The following statements are about what Christians believe about Jesus. But they are all wrong. You need to work out why.

1. *Jesus was God. He looked human but he wasn't really human.*
2. *Jesus was half human, half God.*
3. *When Jesus died, his human side died. Jesus rose from the dead as God. He was once a human being; now he's just God.*
4. *Jesus was God, so he was all powerful.*
5. *Jesus knew everything. He was God, so he knew everything God knows.*
6. *Jesus is not God; he's just the Son of God.*
7. *Jesus is God the Father.*
8. *Jesus is God the Holy Spirit.*
9. *God the Son became a man as Jesus. Jesus is therefore one third of God.*
10. *The idea that God became a human being as Jesus is called the doctor of the reincarnation.*
11. *Jesus did not really die on the cross. He is God, and God cannot die.*

Baptism

Any religious ritual which involves bathing in water can be called 'baptism'. Literally, it means 'to be submerged'. The Essenes and John the Baptist practiced baptism, but Christian baptism is different from both.

In Matthew's Gospel, the risen Jesus commanded his followers: 'Go therefore and make disciples of all nations, baptising them in the name of the Father and of the Son and of the Holy Spirit.'

The basic ceremony is the same in any church. The person is immersed in water, or has water poured over his or her head, with the words, 'I baptise you in the name of the Father, and of the Son, and of the Holy Spirit.'

Most Christians, in fact, practise infant baptism: they baptise babies. This practice goes back at least to the second century.

However, it's not clear that the very *first* Christians baptised people as babies. As a result, some Christians decided that baptism should only be for adults. This happened at the Reformation in the sixteenth century, when some theologians wanted to recapture what they saw as the purity of the earliest Church. The New Testament, especially the Acts of the Apostles, only directly mentions baptism for adults.

As a result, many Protestant Churches – though not all – have **adult baptism** only. This is also called **believer's baptism**.

Churches which have infant baptism include the Roman Catholic Church, the Anglican Church (Church of England, Church of Wales, Church of Ireland and the same Church throughout the world), the Orthodox, and the Lutheran Church.

(It's important to remember that these Churches *do* allow adult baptism as well, for people who were not baptised when they were infants.)

Churches which only have adult baptism include the Baptists, the Amish, and many independent Protestant Churches.

Roman Catholics, Anglicans and the Orthodox say that baptism is a sacrament: a sign of something that God is doing. When someone is baptised, God welcomes that person into the Christian community, and makes him or her a member of the Kingdom of God.

Baptists disagree with this view. Baptism, they say, is a sign of something God has *already* done: giving someone faith. A baby is too young to have faith and so babies cannot be baptised.

Believer's baptism:

The exact details vary between different communities, but the following general points can be made:

- Baptism is carried out either by a member of the community or by the minister or pastor.
- The person to be baptised (or 'candidate') sometimes gives a testimony: a short talk telling others why they became a Christian.
- The words of baptism are used ('I baptise you in the name of the Father, and of the Son, and of the Holy Spirit').
- Baptism is by total immersion: the candidate is submerged in water and is then pulled back up. This symbolizes 'dying and rising with Christ', a key idea in the letters of Paul in the New Testament.
- The baptistery – a pool – is either a temporary structure or one permanently available.

Infant baptism

In the Anglican and Roman Catholic Churches, Christians are usually baptised as babies, and make their adult commitment, if they wish, by being *confirmed*. Confirmation confirms membership of the Church. The Roman Catholic Church usually confirms people at around age fifteen. The Anglican Church usually confirms people slightly younger.

The Orthodox Church combines baptism and confirmation into one ceremony called *chrismation*. Babies are chrismated.

In the Anglican and Roman Catholic Churches, there is a service of baptism, which is generally combined with the Eucharist. The priest or deacon welcomes everyone, prayers are said, and the parents and godparents are invited to gather round the font, a structure like a large basin on a pedestal. (Some fonts in British churches can be as much as a thousand years old, so they've seen quite a few baptisms!) The godparents are friends of the family or relatives, who promise to help bring the child up as a Christian.

Baptism is usually not by total immersion (though it can be); it's more normal for the water to be poured on the baby's head, three times, when each person of the Trinity is mentioned. This is the point at which *Christian names* are given: the priest or deacon will say the child's Christian names (not the surname), and then continue, 'I baptise you in the name of the Father, and of the Son, and of the Holy Spirit.'

Revision tip:

A popular topic for the exam is to ask whether you think babies should be baptised, or whether people should receive believer's baptism. The table on the next page gives the main arguments and they're worth learning. You won't have time to use all of them in the exam, so it's best to concentrate on two rather than try to cram them all in.

People should wait until they're adults before they're baptised	Babies should be baptised.
The earliest Christians baptised only adults, so Christians today should do the same.	This isn't certain, in fact. Although Acts mentions adults being baptised, it also says people were baptised 'with their whole households', which must have included children.
You need to wait until you're older before you can make your own decision about your religion.	Yes, but confirmation allows people to do that. And parents have to make lots of decisions on their children's behalf. You can't wait until a child is ready to feed herself before you give her any food!
Baptism is about faith. A tiny child is a child of God, but has no faith. So you must wait until later.	It depends what you think baptism's for. If God welcomes people into the Church by baptism, then why deny it to children?
The idea of baptising babies is a later development. We have to go back to what the New Testament Church was like.	Most Christians, for over 1800 years, have baptised babies. Jesus loved children. Wouldn't he have wanted them to be baptised too?

The Eucharist / The Mass

Nearly all Christians re-enact the Last Supper in a church service as part of their worship. A name most Christians would accept for this type of service is the *Eucharist*. This comes from a Greek word meaning 'to give thanks'. So, 'Eucharist' means 'thanksgiving'.

Different Christians have different names for the Eucharist:

- The Mass (Roman Catholics and some Anglicans: members of the Church of England, Church of Wales and Church of Ireland);
- Holy Communion (Anglicans and Methodists);
- The Lord's Supper (Anglicans and some Protestants);
- The Liturgy (Orthodox);
- The Breaking of Bread (a name found in the New Testament (Acts 2.42), used by the Brethren and some other Protestants)

In the **Roman Catholic, Orthodox and Anglican Churches**, the Eucharist is celebrated frequently. The service has to be taken by a priest. (Bishops, including the Pope and archbishops, are also priests, so they too can preside over or 'celebrate' the Eucharist.)

Catholics, Orthodox and Anglicans Christians are meant to go to the Eucharist or Mass every Sunday and on the great holy days of the Church's year. Catholics, the Orthodox and some (though not all) Anglicans believe that the bread and the wine of the Eucharist undergo a *change*. They become a channel of God's love: a sacrament. They still appear to be bread and wine, but genuinely become the body and blood of the risen Jesus. Jesus becomes present in them: they are far more than a reminder of him.

In the first century, 'my body' and 'my blood' both meant 'my *self*'. It's a misunderstanding to think that the bread becomes Jesus' corpse, or that the wine becomes Jesus' blood plasma, red and white blood cells and haemoglobin. **Both bread and wine become Jesus himself.**

Eating the 'bread' and drinking the 'wine' enable Christians to have a genuine meeting with the risen Jesus himself.

And the idea that Jesus is genuinely present in the bread and wine is called the doctrine of the **real presence.** It is understood in different ways in different churches.

The risen Jesus is present in the same way in the bread as in the wine. (For this reason, Roman Catholics *sometimes* only receive the 'bread' – they communicate 'in one kind'. This custom developed about 1000 years ago. It is much less common now, although it still happens. Normally, though, Roman Catholics receive both 'bread' and 'wine'.)

A great deal of ritual has grown up around the Eucharist for those who believe in the real presence. The ritual emphasises how holy it is; meeting Jesus at the Eucharist is not something casual but something of supreme importance. There may be special robes for the priest ('vestments'), candles and incense. The wine is contained in a chalice (which looks rather like a goblet) and the plate for the bread is called a paten. They may be made of precious metal. Or they may be plainer; Jesus, after all, was far from rich and would have used an inexpensive cup and plate. So, they may just be made of steel or pottery.

The point at which the bread and wine become the body and blood of Christ is called the **consecration**. This happens when the priest repeats Jesus' words, 'This is my body' and 'This is my blood'.

Christians who believe in the real presence treat the 'bread' and 'wine' after the consecration with great respect. Any 'wine' left after communion is consumed, usually by the priest. Any 'bread' left is either consumed or is placed in a special cupboard in the church called a 'tabernacle'. Christians who believe in the real presence will often use the bread and wine to help to focus their worship in church:

- They may genuflect – go down on one knee – to the tabernacle or to the host (the 'bread') and
- They may pray in front of the host.

The Eucharist is usually seen by **Protestant Christianity** (some Anglicans, the United Reformed Church, Baptists, Methodists, the Church of Scotland, the Free Churches) more as a **commemoration** or **memorial** of Jesus' death.

(Some Protestants, such as the Lutherans, *do* accept the real presence, so it is a mistake to say all Protestants reject it.)

For these Christians, the Eucharist is celebrated less often than in Catholic or Orthodox churches. These Christians do not believe that the bread and wine change in any way; instead they symbolize Christians' unity with Christ in his death and in his resurrection. They also symbolize the fellowship between Christians. The Eucharist is often celebrated with moving simplicity in church, or in 'house groups' in people's homes. Some independent churches have grown too large to meet in normal houses; they'll often hire school or community halls on Sunday mornings.

Some Protestant Eucharists are more like the Catholic Mass than others. This is true of the Methodists, where the service has to be led by a minister. Anglicans who do not believe in the real presence still follow the same wording for the service as other Anglicans, though there is less ritual and the emphasis in the service is different.

In independent churches, the service does not always have to be led by a minister.

There are over 2000 Protestant denominations and it's difficult to generalise. However, this is what can be said:

- Belief in the real presence is usually rejected.

- The ritual for the Eucharist is far less elaborate and it is held less often.
- The Eucharist is about *remembering* Jesus and what he did. The bread and wine are not Jesus himself, but they do symbolise him.

Receiving communion

Exam questions are sometimes asked on how this is done. 'Receiving communion' or 'communicating' means consuming the 'bread' and 'wine'. Different Christians receive communion in different ways:

- Anglicans usually kneel; Roman Catholics usually stand. The host ('bread') is received in the hand or directly into the mouth. The 'wine' is drunk from a shared chalice.
- Some Protestants remain in their seats and are served with bread and individual glasses of wine (which may be non alcoholic; in the Catholic, Anglican and Orthodox Churches, though, the wine has to be alcoholic).
- The Orthodox receive the 'bread' and 'wine' together; they're given by the priest on a long handled spoon.

Revision tip

When writing about Protestant Christians, remember there's no such thing as 'the Protestant Church'; there are over 2000 denominations. So it's always best to put the word 'some' in front of 'Protestant' in the exam. Don't write 'Protestants believe that...'; always write 'some Protestants believe that...'!

Also, be careful about calling Anglicans 'Protestants'. While some Anglicans see themselves as Protestants, others believe very strongly that they are not: they would see themselves as Catholics (although not Roman Catholics because they do not accept the authority of the Pope). Catholic minded Anglicans – 'Anglo Catholics' as they're called – actually form the majority of Anglicans worldwide.

For GCSE, then, it's best just to say 'Anglicans' rather than lumping them together with 'Protestants'.

Persecution and Christianity today

A key theme in Mark is persecution. Scholars usually think that Mark's Church was among those persecuted by Nero. Some exam boards want candidates to know about the persecution of Christians in the modern world.

Lots of governments don't like religion, and they persecute religious people. More widespread is victimization of religious people by individuals and groups who are not backed by governments.

We'll look at a few examples. Just looking at a few seems heartless, as though it ignores the suffering of others, but so many people are under attack that, if we were to cover all of them, this book would run into thousands of pages. But here are a few cases, from the end of the first decade of the twenty-first century.

- **In the Eastern Indian state of Orissa,** violence against Christians has been going on for years. Criminal damage of churches is common; in 2007, nearly twenty churches were destroyed. Christians' houses have been torched; many Christians have been killed. The persecution is led by extremist Hindus. Most Hindus want nothing to do with this sort of outrage and the attacks have been condemned by the Indian government.

- In **Eritrea** in Africa, religion is strictly controlled. There are government approved Muslim, Orthodox, Catholic and Lutheran bodies, but people who want to worship God outside these groups are arrested. It is illegal for two Christians to meet together to pray, if their Church is not approved by the government. In 2008, more than 2000 Christians were in prison for their faith; some had been in jail for years. None of them had had a trial. One house church pastor was arrested and imprisoned; the government then came for his wife and small children. They were locked up in a metal shipping container for three weeks. Other Christians suffer similar or worse ill treatment in Eritrean prisons.

- Many **asylum seekers** in the UK are Christians from Eritrea or other countries who are fleeing persecution.

Mark and community cohesion

The United Kingdom contains many cultures and many religions. For the sake of social harmony, it's important that they get along.

Today, religious intolerance continues. People from different backgrounds can be suspicious of each other.

One solution to this is simply the concept of tolerance or, better still, *agape*: the type of love Jesus commanded everyone to have for other people. If people treated others as they would like to be treated themselves, there would be no social strife. Racism and any other forms of cruelty would be completely ruled out. Different communities would get along well.

The following passages in Mark could be applied to social and community cohesion today:

- The arguments about the Sabbath could be applied to today by saying religious laws should not divide people. Human beings are more important than rituals (2.23-3.6).

- What is inside a person is more important than what is outside (7.18 -23). This could be applied to today by saying one should not judge from appearances.

- Jesus' eating with people who were considered bad characters could be applied to today by saying people from different backgrounds should get along. It's fine to socialise with people from different communities; indeed, it should be encouraged (2.15-17).

- There are limits, though. Christians are not just commanded to love, they're also commanded to hate what is evil. Many religions, including Christianity, contain extremists who are prepared to hate and even to kill for their beliefs. While Christians should be concerned for the welfare of people who have dangerous ideas, they're not called on to tolerate those ideas. In Mark, Jesus would not allow the abuses he saw in the Temple (11.15-18).

- Neither can Christians throw their hands up in horror at the wickedness of the world and retreat into cosy little ghettoes. They have to render unto Caesar the things that are Caesar's, to take a responsible part in society (12.13-17)

Test yourself questions:
How well do you know
Mark's Gospel?

You won't need to know all of these! Check your exam board's specification to see which passages they set. You can do this online.

Introduction (Mark 1.1)
1. In the first verse of Mark, what kind of message describes the book?
2. In the first verse of Mark, which two titles are given to Jesus?

The preaching of John the Baptist (1.2-8)
3. Which prophet predicted John's arrival?
4. In the prophecy, what is the voice (or 'someone') shouting? Where is it shouting?
5. Where did John first appear?
6. People came out to hear John. Where did they come from?
7. In which river did John baptise?
8. What did John wear?
9. What did he eat?
10. John predicted someone would come after him. John said he was not good enough even to – what?
11. When this person arrived, what would he baptise the people with?

Jesus' baptism and temptation (1.9-11)
12. Jesus came to John to be baptised. From which town did he come?
13. What did Jesus see the heavens do?
14. How did the Holy Spirit descend?
15. What did the voice from heaven say?
16. Where was Jesus tempted?
17. Who made him go there?
18. Who tempted him?
19. How long was he there?

Jesus calls the first disciples (1.14-20)
20. When did Jesus go to preach the good news in Galilee?
21. What was his message?
22. Where did Jesus meet the first four disciples?
23. The first four disciples were Simon, Andrew, James and John.
a) Identify the two pairs of brothers.
b) The name of the father of one of the pairs is given. What was his name and who was he?

24. What did they do for a living?
25. What did Jesus say to the first pair he met?
26. When Jesus called them, did they hang around before they followed him?

The first miracle in Mark (1.21-28)
27. In which building in which town did this miracle take place?
28. What day of the week was it?
29. Why were the people amazed at Jesus' teaching?
30. A man who had a demon shouted at Jesus. What did he shout?
31. What did Jesus say to the demon?
32. What did the demon do before it left the man?
33. What was the people's reaction?

Jesus heals Simon Peter's mother in law (1.29-31)
34. What was wrong with her?
35. How did Jesus heal her?
36. What did she do after she was cured?

The healing of many people (1.32-34)
37. The people brought to Jesus all the sick and those who were possessed by demons. At what time of day was this?
38. Where did the people gather?
39. Jesus healed the people and drove out demons. Why wouldn't he allow the demons to speak?

A preaching tour (1.35-39)
40. Jesus left the house early next morning, before daylight. Where did he go and why?
41. Who found him and what did they say?
42. Jesus said they had to go to the other villages in the area. Why?
43. Where did Jesus preach in Galilee and what did he do?

Jesus heals a leper (1.40-45)

44. The leper knelt before Jesus. What did he say?
45. How does Mark say Jesus felt about this request?
46. How did Jesus cure him?
47. What did Jesus then tell the man to do?
48. How did he disobey Jesus' request?
49. How did this disobedience affect Jesus?

Jesus heals a paralysed man (2.1-12)

50. Where did this healing take place?
51. Why were the men bringing the paralysed man not able to get him to Jesus?
52. How many men brought the paralysed man?
53. How did they manage to get the paralysed man to Jesus?
54. What did Jesus say to the paralysed man when he saw their faith?
55. Whom did this annoy, and why?
56. How did Jesus prove to them that he had the authority to forgive sins?
57. When Jesus said he had this authority, what did he call himself?
58. The paralysed man picked up his mat and went out. What did the onlookers say?

Jesus calls Levi (2.13-17)

59. Where did Jesus return to?
60. Where was Levi when Jesus called him?
61. What did Jesus say to him?
62. What did Levi do?
63. Who was Levi's father?
64. Later on, with whom was Jesus eating?
65. Who asked the disciples why he ate with people like that?
66. Jesus' reply said something about a doctor. What?

The question about fasting (2.18-22)

67. Who was fasting and who was not?
68. Who asked Jesus about this?
69. In Jesus' reply:
a) What will the wedding guests not do, and for how long?
b) What will happen to the bridegroom, and what will they then do?
c) What do you not do with a piece of new cloth?
d) What happens if you do?
e) What do you not do with new wine?
f) What happens if you do?
g) What do you use for new wine?

The Sabbath corn (2.23-28)

70. Where were Jesus and his disciples walking?
71. Who saw them, and what was their complaint?
72. Whom did Jesus refer to from the Old Testament, and what had he done?
73. Complete the following quotation: 'The _____ was made for the good of _____ _____; they were not made for the _____. So the Son of _____ is _____ even of the Sabbath.

The man with the paralysed hand (3.1-6)

74. Where did Jesus perform this miracle?
75. Some people were watching Jesus closely. What did they want to see?
76. Jesus called the man out and asked whether or not the Torah allowed one to save a man's life on the Sabbath. What was the reaction and how did Jesus feel about this?
77. What did Jesus say to the man to heal him?
78. After this incident, which two groups began to plot Jesus' death?

The crowd on the seashore (3.7-12)

79. Give two places the crowd came from.
80. How did Jesus avoid being crushed by the crowd?
81. Jesus healed people. What did the demons say when they were exorcised, and what did Jesus forbid them to do?

Jesus chooses the twelve (3.13-19)

82. Where did Jesus go to call the twelve?
83. What did Jesus call the twelve?
84. What three things were the twelve to do?
85. Name the twelve.
86. Who were the Boanerges and what does the word mean?

Is he evil or just insane? (3.20-35)

87. Jesus went home and a large crowd gathered. They had no time to – what?
88. When his family heard about it, what did they say?
89. Where had the teachers of the Law (scribes) come from?
90. Where did they say Jesus' power to drive out demons came from?
91. Jesus showed their view was silly by speaking of a country and a family. What did he say?
92. If you want to steal a strong man's belongings, what do you have to do first?
93. What is the unforgivable sin, and why did Jesus mention it?

94. Who did Jesus say were his mother, brother or sister?

The parable of the sower and the purpose of the parables (4.1-20)
95. Where did Jesus preach this parable?
96. What happened to the seed that fell along the path?
97. What happened to the seed that fell on rocky ground?
98. What happened to the seed that fell among thorn bushes?
99. What happened to the seed that fell on good soil?
100. To whom has the secret of the Kingdom of God been given?
101. Who will look and look, yet not see, and listen and listen, yet not understand?
102. If these people could see and understand, what would happen?
103. In the interpretation of the parable, what does the sower sow?
104. What sort of people are like the seeds that fall along the path?
105. What sort of people are like the seeds that fall on rocky ground?
106. What sort of people are like the seeds that fall among the thorn bushes?
107. What sort of people are like the seeds that produce corn?

More parables (4.21-34)
108. Where should you not put a lamp?
109. Where should you put it?
110. What will happen to things that are hidden and things that are covered up?
111. What will be the measure you give?
112. What will happen to people who have something?
113. What will happen to people who have nothing?
114. Does the man who plants seed know how it grows?
115. What does the man do when the corn is ripe?
116. How big is a mustard seed?
117. What does it become?
118. What happens in its shade?
119. To whom did Jesus always explain the parables?

The calming of the storm (4.35-41)
120. What time of day was it when they set off for the other side of the Sea of Galilee?
121. What happened to the boat when the strong wind blew up?

122. Where and on what was Jesus sleeping?
123. When the disciples woke him, what did they say?
124. What did Jesus say to the wind?
125. What did Jesus say to the waves?
126. What did he then say to the disciples?
127. Why were the disciples then afraid?

The madman in the tombs (5.1-20)
128. Where did the boat land?
129. Where did the demoniac live?
130. Why was he no longer chained up?
131. What did he do day and night?
132. He ran to meet Jesus. What did he say at first?
133. What did the man say his name was, and why?
134. What did the spirits beg Jesus?
135. What happened to the pigs, and how many were there?
136. When the news spread around, what did the locals ask Jesus to do?
137. What did the man who was healed want to do?
138. What did Jesus tell him to do instead?
139. Where did the man spread the message about Jesus?

Jairus' daughter and the woman who touched Jesus' cloak (5.21-43)
140. What was Jairus' job?
141. What was wrong with his daughter?
142. What did Jairus ask Jesus to do?
143. What was wrong with the woman who was ill and how long had she suffered from this?
144. Had the doctors been able to help?
145. Why did she want to touch Jesus' clothes?
146. How did Jesus know he had been touched?
147. The woman told Jesus what had happened. What did he say to her?
148. What did the messengers from Jairus' house then say?
149. Who did Jesus take with him to Jairus' house?
150. Jesus said the child was not dead, but – what?
151. Who did Jesus take with him into the room where the girl was, and who did he get to leave?
152. What did Jesus say to raise the girl and what does this mean?
153. When she got up, what did Jesus tell her to do?
154. How old was she?

Jesus is rejected at Nazareth (6.1-6)

155. Where and when did Jesus teach in Nazareth?
156. The local people rejected Jesus because they knew him and his family. Name:
    a) Jesus' mother
    b) Jesus' brothers.
157. What was Jesus' job said to be?
158. Where and by whom did Jesus say a prophet is never respected?
159. What could Jesus not do there?
160. What astonished Jesus?

Jesus sends out the twelve (6.7-13)

161. How many disciples travelled together?
162. Over what did Jesus give them authority?
163. What were they to carry to help them walk?
164. What could they not take?
165. Where should they stay?
166. What sign should they give as a warning to places that did not welcome them?
167. The twelve cast out demons. How did they heal the sick?

The death of John the Baptist (6.14-29)

168. Who did Herod think Jesus was?
169. Name Herod's wife.
170. Why had Herod imprisoned John?
171. When was there a celebration for Herod?
172. Who danced?
173. What did Herod promise her?
174. What did her mother tell her to ask for?
175. Why could Herod not refuse?
176. What happened to John's body?

The feeding of the 5000 (6.30-44)

177. Why did Jesus suggest to the disciples that they should go to a lonely place?
178. People followed them. Why did Jesus have compassion on them?
179. The disciples told Jesus to send the people away to buy food. What did he say to them?
180. What food did the disciples have?
181. How is the grass described?
182. When the people sat down, how big was each group?
183. How many baskets were filled with the leftovers of the meal?

The walking on the water (6.45-52)

184. Where did Jesus send the boat to?
185. What did Jesus do once he had dismissed the crowd?
186. At what time did Jesus walk towards the disciples on the water?

187. What did they think he was?
188. What did Jesus say to reassure them?
189. What happened to the weather when Jesus got into the boat?
190. What could the disciples still not understand?

Jesus heals the sick in Gennesaret (6.53-56)

191. Where did they land?
192. What were the sick people lying on?
193. What did they want to touch?

What makes a person unclean? (7.1-23)

194. Where had the Pharisees and scribes come from?
195. What had the disciples been doing to break the Law?
196. What were the Pharisees' regulations about ritual washing?
197. Which prophet did Jesus say predicted the Pharisees' hypocrisy?
198. What did the Pharisees put aside, and what do they obey?
199. What is Corban, and why did Jesus condemn it?
200. What did Jesus say cannot defile someone (make him or her ritually unclean)?
201. To whom did Jesus have to explain this?
202. Why did he say things which enter you from outside do not defile you?
203. Mark says Jesus abolished part of the Torah by this. Which part?
204. What does Jesus say defiles a person? Give examples.

The Syro-Phoenician woman (7.24-30)

205. Where did Jesus go for this story?
206. What was wrong with the woman's daughter?
207. Where did the woman come from?
208. Was she a Jew or a Gentile?
209. When she asked Jesus to heal her daughter, what did he say about bread and dogs?
210. What did she say in reply?
211. What did the woman find when she returned home, as Jesus had promised?

The deaf mute (7.31-37)

212. Jesus then went towards the Sea of Galilee. What route did he then take?
213. How did Jesus heal the man?
214. What did Jesus say and what does it mean?
215. What did Jesus order the people to do?
216. Did they obey him?
217. Why were the people amazed?

The feeding of the 4000 (8.1-10)

218. What food did the disciples have?
219. How many baskets of scraps were left over?

The Pharisees ask for a sign, the yeast of the Pharisees and Herod (8.11-21)

220. Did Jesus agree to the Pharisees' request?
221. What had the disciples forgotten?
222. Jesus warned them of the yeast (leaven) of the Pharisees and of Herod. What did they think he meant?
223. What did Jesus remind them of?

The blind man at Bethsaida (8.22-26)

224. Where did this healing take place?
225. Where did Jesus take the blind man?
226. What did he do to the man's eyes?
227. What did people look like to him?
228. When he was healed, what did Jesus forbid him to do?

Who do you say I am? (Peter's confession) (8.27-9.1)

229. Which town were Jesus and the disciples near?
230. Who did people think Jesus was?
231. Who did Peter say Jesus was?
232. Jesus taught that the Son of Man must be rejected. By whom?
233. What would happen three days after he is put to death?
234. Who rebuked him for saying this?
235. What did Jesus say to him?
236. Jesus told the crowd that anyone who wants to follow him must – what?
237. What will happen to people who want to save their lives?
238. What will happen to people who lose their lives for the sake of Jesus and for the gospel?
239. Complete the following: 'What good is it for a man to gain the whole _____, yet forfeit his _____?'
240. What will happen to the person who is ashamed of Jesus and of his teaching?
241. Some standing there will not taste death until they see – what?

The Transfiguration (9.2-13)

242. How much later than the previous incident did the Transfiguration take place?
243. Who did Jesus take with him?
244. Where did they go?
245. Jesus' clothes became whiter than – what?
246. Who appeared to Jesus?

247. Who wanted to make what?
248. What overshadowed them?
249. What did the voice from heaven say?
250. When were the disciples allowed to tell what they had seen?
251. Who do the scribes say should come before the Messiah?
252. Had this person in fact come?

Jesus heals an epileptic boy (9.14-29)

253. Who was arguing with the crowd and the disciples?
254. Who asked Jesus to heal the boy?
255. Who had failed to heal him?
256. What made the boy epileptic?
257. What happened when they brought the boy to Jesus?
258. How long had the condition lasted?
259. For whom is everything possible?
260. When Jesus healed the boy, what did the boy look like at first?
261. The disciples asked Jesus why they could not perform the cure. What drives out this sort of demon?

The second passion prediction
Who is the greatest? (9.30-37)

262. What was Jesus teaching his disciples as they went through Galilee?
263. How did they respond to this teaching?
264. What had the disciples been arguing about on the road?
265. What should the person who wants to be first become?
266. If people welcome children in Jesus' name, who do they welcome?
267. If people welcome Jesus, who do they also welcome?

'Whoever is not against us is for us'
Temptations to sin
Salt (9.38-50)

268. Who saw a man driving out demons in Jesus' name?
269. Anyone who is not against Jesus is – what?
270. Who will certainly receive his reward?
271. For whom will it be better to have a millstone tied round his neck and be thrown into the sea?
272. If your right hand causes you to sin, what should you do?
273. If your foot causes you to sin, what should you do?
274. If your eye causes you to sin, what should you do?

275. It is better to enter life maimed than to go – where?
276. What do worms never do?
277. What never happens to the fire?
278. Everything will be salted (purified) with – what?
279. When is it implied that salt is no good?
280. What should the disciples have in themselves to live in peace with one another?

Jesus' teaching on divorce (10.1-12)
281. Who asked Jesus whether the Law allows a man to divorce his wife?
282. What did Moses allow?
283. Why did Jesus say Moses allowed the Jews to do this?
284. Why does Mark say Jesus did not allow divorce?
285. What did Jesus say a man is doing if he divorces his wife and marries again?
286. What did Jesus say a woman is doing if she divorces her husband and marries again?

Children and the Kingdom (10.13-16)
287. What did Jesus say belongs to the children?
288. What will happen to the person who does not receive the Kingdom of God like a child?

The rich man (10.17-31)
289. What did the rich man ask Jesus?
290. Who did Jesus say was good?
291. What did Jesus tell the man to keep?
292. How long had the man kept these?
293. What did Jesus then tell him to do?
294. What was the rich man's reaction to this?
295. Complete the following: 'It is easier for a _____ to go through the _____ of a _____ than for a _____ man to enter the _____ of _____.'
296. How did the disciples react to this, and what did they ask each other?
297. What is impossible for God?
298. What did Peter remind Jesus that they had left to follow him?
299. What will such people receive
   a) now, and
   b) in the age to come,
   according to Jesus?
300. What will happen to many who are first, and to many who are last?

The third passion prediction (10.32-34)
301. Where were Jesus and the disciples heading?
302. Who will condemn the Son of Man to death?

303. To whom will they hand him over?
304. What will they do to the Son of Man when they receive him?
305. What will happen on the third day?

James and John's question (10.35-45)
306. What did James and John ask?
307. What will they drink and be washed with?
308. How did the other disciples react to the brothers' request?
309. Who should the disciples not be like?
310. What should they do to be great?
311. What should they do to be first?
312. What did the Son of Man come to do and to give?

Bartimaeus (10.46-52)
313. What was wrong with Bartimaeus?
314. Where did he live?
315. What did he call Jesus when he shouted out to him?
316. What did Jesus say had made Bartimaeus well?
317. What did he do once he was cured?

Jesus enters Jerusalem in triumph (11.1-11)
318. As they approached Jerusalem, they came to a mountain, near two towns. Which mountain and which towns?
319. What did Jesus say the disciples would find in the village?
320. What were they to say if anyone asked them what they were doing?
321. When the disciples brought the animal to Jesus, what did they throw on it?
322. What did the people spread on the road?
323. What did the people shout?
324. Where did Jesus go in Jerusalem?
325. As it was late, where did they then go?

The cursing of the fig tree
The cleansing of the Temple (11.12-25)
326. Why were there no figs on the tree?
327. What did Jesus say to the tree?
328. Who did Jesus drive out of the Temple?
329. What did he overturn?
330. What did he prevent them doing in the Temple courtyards?
331. What is the Temple for all nations?
332. What had they made it?
333. What did the chief priests and the scribes do when they heard of this?
334. Why were they afraid of him?
335. What had happened to the fig tree next morning?
336. What did Jesus say about throwing a mountain (or hill) into the sea?

337. If you ask for something in prayer and believe you have received it, what will happen?
338. When you stand and pray, and forgive others, what will God do?

What do you think you're doing? (The question about authority) (11.27-33)
339. Who asked Jesus where his authority came from?
340. Where did this take place?
341. What did Jesus ask them in return?
342. Why could they not answer?
343. What answer did they eventually give Jesus?
344. What did Jesus then refuse to tell them?

The allegory of the vineyard (12.1-12)
345. What did the man who planted the vineyard dig, and what did he build?
346. What was the owner's slave sent to collect?
347. What did the tenants do to this first servant?
348. What did they do to the next slave?
349. What did they do to the third slave, and to the slaves after that?
350. Who did the owner finally send?
351. Why did the tenants kill this person?
352. What did they do with the body?
353. What will the owner of the vineyard do?
354. What will happen to the stone the builders rejected?
355. Why did the Jewish leaders try to arrest Jesus?
356. Why did they leave him alone?

The question about paying taxes (12.13-17)
357. Who asked Jesus about paying taxes?
358. To whom did the taxes go?
359. Whose head was on the denarius (coin)?
360. What should they give to Caesar?
361. What should they give to God?

The question about the resurrection (12.18-27)
362. Who asked Jesus about this?
363. What does the Law of Moses say about looking after widows?
364. In their story, how many brothers were there?
365. What did all the brothers do?
366. What was the punchline, which was designed to make belief in the resurrection look silly?
367. What did Jesus say they did not know?
368. When the dead rise to life, what will they be like?

369. What will they then not do?
370. What did God say in the passage about the bush?
371. God is not God of the dead, but – what?

The greatest commandment (12.28-34)
372. Who asked Jesus about this?
373. Which two commandments did Jesus say were the greatest?
374. The scribe agreed that these two commandments were more important than – what?
375. What did Jesus say the scribe was not far from?

The question about the Messiah (12.35-37)
376. Who asked how the scribes could say the Christ was the Son of David?
377. What did David call the Christ in the psalm?

The scribes (12.37b-40)
378. What do the scribes like to wear?
379. What do they have in synagogues?
380. What will they receive?

The widow's offering (12.41-44)
381. Where did the widow make her offering?
382. How much did she give?
383. Why, according to Jesus, had she given more than the rich men?

The end of the world (the apocalyptic discourse) (Mark 13)
384. What will happen to the Temple?
385. Where did Jesus deliver this speech?
386. Who will deceive many people?
387. What must happen before the end?
388. When the disciples are arrested and taken to court, who will help them to speak?
389. What will children do to their parents?
390. What will happen to the person who holds out to the end?
391. When they see the desolating sacrilege (the 'abomination of desolation' or the 'awful horror'), what should those in Judea do?
392. What should a man on his roof not do?
393. People should pray to God that the end will not happen – when?
394. Why has God shortened the days of suffering?
395. Who will appear?
396. What will happen to the sun and moon?
397. On what will the Son of Man return?
398. What will the angels do?
399. When the fig tree puts forth its leaves, what does it show?

400. Heaven and earth will pass away. What will not pass away?
401. The Son and the angels do not know when the end will be. Who does?
402. What should the disciples do, since they do not know when the time will come?
403. If the master of the house comes suddenly, what should he not find the disciples doing?

The plot against Jesus and Jesus' anointing (14.1-11)
404. The chief priests and the scribes plotted against Jesus. This was two days before a festival. Which one?
405. Why did they not want to arrest Jesus during the festival?
406. In which town was Jesus anointed?
407. Whose house was Jesus eating in?
408. What was the woman's ointment made from?
409. Why were some of the people angry?
410. What did Jesus say about the poor?
411. Why did Jesus say the woman had anointed his body?
412. What did the Jewish leaders agree to give Judas?

The last supper (14.12-31)
413. Who would show the disciples the place for them to eat the Passover meal with Jesus?
414. Which day of the festival was this, and what did the Jews do then?
415. One of the twelve would dip his bread in the dish with Jesus. Which one would that be?
416. What did Jesus say the bread was?
417. What did Jesus say the wine was?
418. What did Jesus' blood seal?
419. When would Jesus next drink wine?
420. After they had sung a hymn, where did they go?
421. What did Jesus predict the disciples would all do?
422. Which disciple said he would not?
423. When Jesus was raised to life, where would he go before the disciples to?
424. What would happen before the cock crowed twice?

Jesus in Gethsemane (14.32-52)
425. Who did Jesus take with him?
426. What did Jesus call God in his prayer?
427. What did he ask God to do?
428. What were the disciples doing while Jesus was praying?

429. How many times did he find them like this?
430. With whom did Judas arrive?
431. What was the sign Judas would give to identify Jesus to the crowd?
432. Who attacked whom?
433. Who ran away naked?

Jesus' trial before the Sanhedrin (14.53-65)
434. Where did Peter go?
435. Did the witnesses against Jesus agree?
436. What was the accusation against Jesus about the Temple?
437. The high priest asked Jesus if he had any answer to the accusations. What did Jesus say in reply?
438. The high priest then asked him, 'Are you the Messiah, the Son of the Blessed God?' What was Jesus' reply?
439. What did the high priest tear?
440. Of what crime was Jesus found guilty?
441. How did they mock Jesus?

Peter denies Jesus (14.66-72)
442. Who first recognised Peter?
443. What happened immediately after Peter first said he did not know Jesus?
444. What made the bystanders sure that Peter was a disciple?
445. What did Peter do when the cock crowed a second time?

Jesus' trial before Pilate
446. Give Pilate's first name.
447. Before they handed Jesus over to Pilate, what did the Sanhedrin do first thing in the morning?
448. What was the first question Pilate asked Jesus?
449. What was Jesus' reply?
450. The chief priests accused Jesus of many things. Pilate asked him if he was going to answer them. What did Jesus say?
451. Who was Barabbas?
452. The governor used to set free one prisoner as a favour to the Jews. At what time of the year did he do this?
453. What did Pilate ask the crowd?
454. Who did the crowd ask for?
455. Why did they ask for him?
456. What did they want done with Jesus?
457. Why did Pilate give in to them?
458. What happened to Jesus before he was handed over for crucifixion?
459. How did Pilate's soldiers mock Jesus?

The crucifixion (15.21-41)

460. Who was Simon of Cyrene?
461. Name the place where Jesus was crucified, and give its meaning.
462. What was Jesus offered as a painkiller?
463. Did he take it?
464. What did the soldiers do about Jesus' clothes?
465. What time was it when Jesus was crucified?
466. Give the wording of the notice above Jesus' head.
467. Who was crucified with Jesus?
468. What were the insults of
    a) the passers-by?
    b) the chief priests and scribes?
469. When did the darkness start to cover the land, and how long did it last?
470. What did Jesus cry, and what does it mean?
471. Who did people think he was calling?
472. What was Jesus offered on a sponge?
473. Why was he offered this?
474. Jesus died. What happened in the Temple?
475. When the centurion saw how Jesus died, what did he say?
476. Who was looking on from a distance?

Jesus' burial (15.42-47)

477. Who provided Jesus' tomb?
478. What was he looking for (or waiting for)?
479. What was he a member of?
480. When did he ask Pilate for Jesus' body?
481. Why was Pilate surprised?
482. Who saw where Jesus was laid?

The resurrection (16.1-8)

483. Why did the women go to the tomb?
484. When did they go there?
485. What was worrying them on the way?
486. Who did they meet in the tomb?
487. What was the message to the disciples and to Peter?
488. Why did the women keep silent about this?

The longer ending of Mark (added in the second century) (16.9-20)

489. To whom did the risen Jesus first appear?
490. To whom did Jesus appear while they walked in the country?
491. When did Jesus appear to the eleven and why did he scold them?
492. What did he tell them to do?
493. What happened after Jesus had talked with them?

Answers

Note: quotations are usually taken from the Good News Bible.

1. Good news / gospel.
2. Christ, Son of God.
3. Isaiah.
4. The voice shouts an instruction to prepare the Lord's way and to make his paths straight. The voice is said to be shouting in the desert.
5. In the desert.
6. Judea and Jerusalem.
7. The Jordan.
8. Clothes made from camel's hair, leather belt.
9. Locusts and wild honey.
10. Undo his sandal strap.
11. The Holy Spirit.
12. Nazareth.
13. Open.
14. Like a dove.
15. 'You are my own dear Son. I am pleased with you.'
16. The desert.
17. The Spirit.
18. Satan.
19. 40 days.
20. After John had been arrested.
21. 'The right time has come and the Kingdom of God is near! Turn away from your sins and believe the Good News!'
22. By the Sea of Galilee.
23. a) Simon was Andrew's brother; James was John's brother. b) Zebedee
24. Fishermen.
25. Jesus told them to come with him; he would make them catch people.
26. No, they immediately followed him.
27. In the Capernaum synagogue.
28. The Sabbath.
29. They were amazed because he taught them with authority, unlike the scribes.
30. 'What do you want with us, Jesus of Nazareth? Are you here to destroy us? I know who you are – you are God's holy messenger!'
31. 'Be quiet, and come out of the man.'
32. It shook him hard and screamed.
33. They were amazed by Jesus' new teaching and his power over devils, and the news about him spread through Galilee.
34. She had a fever.
35. He took her by the hand and helped her up.
36. She waited on them.
37. That evening after sunset.
38. In front of the house.
39. Because they knew who he was.
40. He went to a lonely place to pray.
41. Simon and his companions found him and said, 'Everyone is looking for you.'
42. He had to preach to them because that was why he came.
43. He preached in the synagogues and drove out demons.
44. 'If you want to, you can make me clean.'
45. He was filled with pity or was angry (the manuscripts of Mark give either).
46. He touched him and said, 'Be clean.'
47. He told the man not to tell anyone, but to go to the priest and offer the sacrifice Moses commanded, as a proof to the people.
48. He spread the news everywhere.
49. He was unable to go into a town publicly, and had to stay in lonely places, where people came to him.
50. Capernaum..
51. Because a crowd had gathered outside the house.
52. Four.
53. They made a hole in the roof and lowered the paralysed man down on his mat.
54. 'My son, your sins are forgiven.'
55. It annoyed the scribes. It was blasphemy; only God could forgive sins.
56. He said to the paralysed man, 'Pick up your mat and go home.'
57. The Son of Man.
58. 'We have never seen anything like this.'
59. The shore of the Sea of Galilee.
60. In his office.
61. 'Follow me.'
62. He got up and followed him.
63. Alphaeus.
64. Levi, other tax collectors and sinners / outcasts, and the disciples.
65. Some scribes who were Pharisees.
66. 'People who are well do not need a doctor, but only those who are sick. I have not come to call respectable people, but outcasts.'
67. The disciples of John the Baptist and the Pharisees were fasting; Jesus and the disciples were not.
68. 'Some people' (unspecified).
69. a) Fast as long as the bridegroom is with them.
b) The bridegroom will be taken away from them and then they will fast.

c) Patch an old garment / coat.

d) The patch will shrink and make an even bigger hole.

e) Put it in old wineskins.

f) The wine will burst the skins and both will be ruined.

g) Fresh wineskins.

70. Through some cornfields.

71. The Pharisees. They complained that Jesus and the disciples were breaking the Law / Torah, since it was the Sabbath.

72. David. He and his men were hungry, so David went into the house of God and ate the ceremonial bread. He also gave some to his men. The Torah said only the priests could eat this bread.

73. 'The Sabbath was made for the good of human beings; they were not made for the Sabbath. So the Son of Man is Lord even of the Sabbath.'

74. In the synagogue.

75. Whether Jesus would heal on the Sabbath.

76. They were silent. Jesus was angry and grieved at their stubbornness.

77. 'Stretch out your hand.'

78. The Pharisees and Herodians (members of Herod's party).

79. Any two from: Galilee, Judea, Jerusalem, Idumea, the East of the Jordan (Transjordan), the area around Tyre and Sidon.

80. He got into a boat.

81. The demons said he was the Son of God. Jesus ordered them not to tell anyone who he was.

82. Up a mountain / hill.

83. Apostles.

84. To be with Jesus, to preach, to cast out devils.

85. Simon Peter, James and John the sons of Zebedee, Andrew, Philip, Bartholomew, Matthew, Thomas, James son of Alphaeus, Thaddaeus, Simon the Zealot / Patriot, Judas Iscariot.

86. James and John. It means 'sons / men of thunder'.

87. Eat.

88. 'He is beside himself' or 'he's mad'.

89. Jerusalem.

90. From Beelzebul.

91. If a county or a family divide themselves into groups, they will fall apart. So if Satan's kingdom divides itself into groups, it is coming to an end.

92. Tie up the strong man.

93. Blasphemy against the Holy Spirit. Jesus mentioned it because they were saying he was possessed.

94. Whoever does the will of God.

95. Jesus was sitting in a boat near the shore of the Sea of Galilee.

96. Birds ate it.

97. It sprouted quickly because the soil was not deep, but it was scorched by the sun.

98. The thorns choked the plants.

99. It grew up and produced 30 grains, 60 grains, and 100 grains.

100. The twelve and those with them.

101. 'Those outside', who do not have the secret of the Kingdom of God.

102. They would turn to God and be forgiven.

103. The word (GNB: God's message).

104. Those who hear the message and immediately it is taken away by Satan.

105. Those who hear the word gladly, but it does not sink in. When persecution comes, they give up.

106. Those in whom the message does not bear fruit because they are so wrapped up in the world.

107. Those who accept the message and bear fruit.

108. Under a bowl or bed.

109. On a lampstand.

110. Hidden things will be brought into the open; things covered up will be uncovered.

111. The message you receive. (The GNB takes this to mean that the rules you use to judge others will be used by God to judge you.)

112. They will be given more.

113. Even what they have will be taken away.

114. No.

115. Harvests it with his sickle.

116. It is the smallest seed in the world.

117. The biggest of all plants.

118. Birds make their nests.

119. To the disciples.

120. Evening.

121. Waves began to fill the boat.

122. In the stern; his head was on a pillow.

123. 'Teacher, don't you care that we are about to die?'

124. 'Be quiet.'

125. 'Be still.'

126. 'Why are you frightened? Have you still no faith?'

127. Because they wondered who Jesus was, when the wind and the waves obeyed him.

128. In the territory of Gerasa / Gadara.
129. Among the tombs.
130. Because he kept smashing the chains.
131. Scream and cut himself with stones.
132. 'Jesus, Son of the Most High God! What do you want with me? For God's sake, I beg you, don't punish me!'
133. Legion (GNB: Mob), because there were so many of them.
134. To let them go into the pigs.
135. They rushed into the lake and were drowned. About 2000.
136. Leave their territory.
137. Go with Jesus.
138. 'Go back home to your family and tell them how much the Lord has done for you and how kind he has been to you.'
139. Throughout the Decapolis / Ten Towns.
140. Ruler / official of the synagogue.
141. She was very ill.
142. Come and lay his hands on her.
143. She had had a severe bleeding for twelve years.
144. No. In fact, she got worse.
145. She thought, 'If I just touch his clothes, I will get well.'
146. He felt the power go out of him.
147. 'My daughter, your faith has made you well. Go in peace, and be healed of your trouble.'
148. Jairus' daughter was dead; there was no point in bothering Jesus further.
149. Peter, James and John.
150. Sleeping.
151. He took with him Peter, James and John and the girl's parents, and got the mourners or bystanders to leave.
152. 'Talitha koum.' 'Little girl, I tell you to get up.'
153. Give her something to eat.
154. 12.
155. In the synagogue on the Sabbath.
156. a) Mary
 b) James, Joseph, Judas, Simon.
157. Carpenter.
158. In his home town, by his relatives and family.
159. Miracles, although he healed a few sick people.
160. Their lack of faith.
161. Two.
162. Evil spirits.
163. A stick.
164. Bread, a beggar's bag, money, an extra tunic / shirt.
165. In one house until they leave the area.
166. Shake the dust from their feet.

167. They anointed them with oil.
168. John the Baptist, raised from the dead.
169. Herodias.
170. Because Herodias wanted him to: John had condemned their marriage, since she was already married to Philip, Herod's brother.
171. On his birthday.
172. Herodias' daughter. (Her name was Salome, but Mark does not mention this.)
173. Anything she wanted, up to half his kingdom.
174. John the Baptist's head on a dish.
175. Because he had made a vow in front of his guests to give the girl what she asked for.
176. His disciples buried it.
177. So they could rest. There were so many people coming and going that they did not even have time to eat.
178. Because they were like sheep without a shepherd.
179. 'You yourselves give them something to eat.'
180. Five loaves, two fish.
181. It was green.
182. Some groups numbers 100, others numbered 50.
183. 12.
184. Bethsaida.
185. He went up a mountain / hill to pray.
186. Between 3 and 6 a.m. / about the fourth watch.
187. A ghost.
188. 'Courage! It is I. Don't be afraid.'
189. The wind died down.
190. About the loaves (the meaning of the feeding miracle).
191. Gennesaret.
192. Mats.
193. The edge of his cloak.
194. Jerusalem.
195. Eating with unwashed hands.
196. To wash hands ritually before eating; to eat nothing from the market without first washing it or wash themselves after coming from the market (the Greek can mean either); to wash cups, pots, copper bowls and beds ritually.
197. Isaiah.
198. They put aide God's commands and obey men's teaching.
199. 'Corban' / 'Korban' means 'devoted to God'. Property or wealth could be declared corban. Some people used it to get round the commandment to honour

their father and mother. This is why Jesus condemned it.
200. What goes into a person from outside.
201. The disciples.
202. Because they do not enter the heart but the stomach, and then pass on.
203. The food laws.
204. A person is defiled by what comes out of him: evil ideas, greed, fornication, theft, evil things, murder, deceit, adultery, indecency, jealousy, slander, pride, folly.
205. To a house near Tyre.
206. She was possessed by a devil.
207. From Phoenicia in Syria.
208. Gentile.
209. 'Let us first feed the children. It isn't right to take the children's food and throw it to the dogs.'
210. 'Sir, even the dogs under the table eat the children's leftovers.'
211. The devil had gone out of her daughter.
212. He went from near Tyre to Sidon, and then through the Decapolis / Ten Towns.
213. He took him away from the crowd, put his fingers in his ears, spat, and touched the man's tongue.
214. Ephphatha. Be opened.
215. Not to talk about it to anyone.
216. No.
217. Because Jesus did everything well, even making the deaf hear and the dumb speak.
218. Seven loaves and a few fish.
219. Seven baskets.
220. No.
221. To bring enough bread.
222. They thought he was talking about their forgetting to bring enough bread.
223. The number of baskets of leftovers after the two feeding miracles.
224. Bethsaida.
225. Out of the village.
226. He spat on them and placed his hands on them.
227. Trees but they are walking.
228. Enter the village.
229. Caesarea Philippi.
230. John the Baptist, Elijah, one of the prophets.
231. The Christ / Messiah.
232. The elders, chief priests and scribes.
233. He will rise.
234. Peter.
235. 'Get away from me, Satan! Your thoughts don't come from God but from human beings!'

236. Forget self and carry his cross.
237. They will lose them.
238. They will save them.
239. 'What good is it for a man to gain the whole world, yet forfeit his soul?'
240. The Son of Man will be ashamed of him when he comes in the glory of his Father with the holy angels.
241. The Kingdom of God come with power.
242. Six days.
243. Peter, James and John.
244. Up a mountain.
245. Anything on earth could bleach them.
246. Elijah and Moses.
247. Peter wanted to make three tents.
248. A cloud.
249. 'This is my own dear Son – listen to him!'
250. When the Son of Man had risen from death.
251. Elijah.
252. Yes, but (it is implied) as John the Baptist.
253. Scribes.
254. His father.
255. The disciples.
256. A demon.
257. The demon threw the boy into a fit.
258. From childhood.
259. For one who has faith.
260. A dead body.
261. Prayer.
262. That the Son of Man would suffer and rise again.
263. They did not understand and were afraid to ask.
264. Who was the greatest.
265. Last and servant of all.
266. Jesus.
267. The one who sent Jesus: God.
268. John.
269. For him.
270. Anyone who gives a disciple a cup of water because he bears the name of Christ.
271. Anyone who causes 'one of these little ones' to sin / lose their faith.
272. Cut it off.
273. Cut it off.
274. Pluck it out.
275. To hell.
276. Die.
277. It is never extinguished.
278. Fire.
279. When it has lost its saltiness.
280. Salt. (The GNB has 'salt of friendship'.)
281. Some Pharisees.

282. Moses allowed a man to give his wife a divorce note and dismiss her.
283. Because of their hardness of heart.
284. Because in the beginning, God made humans male and female. In Genesis, it says, 'for this reason a man will leave his father and mother and unite with his wife, and the two will become one.' They are no longer two, but one. What God has joined, no one must separate.
285. Committing adultery against his wife.
286. Committing adultery against her husband.
287. The Kingdom of God.
288. He shall never enter it.
289. 'Good Teacher, what must I do to inherit eternal life?'
290. No one, except God.
291. The commandments.
292. Since he was young.
293. Sell everything, give the money to the poor and follow Jesus.
294. He went away sad.
295. 'It is easier for a camel to go through the eye of a needle than for a rich man to enter the Kingdom of God.'
296. They were astonished and asked, 'Who, then, can be saved?'
297. Nothing.
298. Everything.
299. a) A hundred times more houses, brothers, sisters, mothers, children, fields and persecutions.
    b) Eternal life.
300. Many who are first will be last; many who are last will be first.
301. Jerusalem.
302. The chief priests and scribes.
303. To the Gentiles.
304. Mock him, spit on him, whip him and kill him.
305. He will rise to life.
306. To sit on Jesus' right and left in the Kingdom.
307. They will drink the cup which Jesus will drink and be washed with the baptism with which Jesus will be washed.
308. They were angry with them.
309. The rulers of the Gentiles.
310. Become the others' servant.
311. Become the slave of all.
312. Not to be served but to serve, and to give his life as a ransom for many.
313. He was blind.
314. Jericho.
315. 'Jesus, Son of David.'
316. His faith.

317. Followed him on the road.
318. The Mount of Olives, Bethphage and Bethany.
319. A colt / donkey tied up, which had never been ridden.
320. The master needs it and will send it back at once.
321. Their cloaks.
322. Their cloaks or branches.
323. 'Praise God!' (or 'Hosanna!') 'God bless him who comes in the name of the Lord! God bless the coming Kingdom of King David, our father! Praise God!' (or 'Hosanna!')
324. To the Temple.
325. To Bethany.
326. It was the wrong time of year.
327. 'No one shall ever eat figs from you again!'
328. Those who were buying and selling.
329. The money-changers' tables and the stools of the pigeon-sellers.
330. Carrying anything through.
331. A house of prayer.
332. A den of thieves.
333. They began to look for a way to kill Jesus.
334. Because the crowd were amazed by his teaching.
335. It had withered.
336. 'I assure you that whoever tells this hill to get up and throw itself into the sea and does not doubt in his heart, but believes that what he says will happen, it will be done for him.'
337. You will be given what you ask for.
338. Forgive you.
339. The chief priests, the scribes and elders.
340. In the Temple.
341. Where did John get his authority to baptise from?
342. Because if they said, 'from God', Jesus would ask why they did not believe him. They could not say, 'from people', because they were afraid of the crowd.
343. 'We don't know.'
344. Where his authority came from
345. He dug a hole for the winepress and he built a watchtower.
346. His share of the harvest.
347. Beat him and sent him away empty-handed.
348. Beat him over the head and treated him shamefully.
349. They killed the third slave and beat and killed the others.
350. His beloved son.

351. So the inheritance would pass to them.
352. Threw it out of the vineyard.
353. Kill the tenants and give the vineyard to others.
354. It became the most important stone of all, the keystone.
355. Because they knew he had told the parable against them.
356. Because they were afraid of the crowd.
357. Some Pharisees and Herodians (members of Herod's party).
358. To Rome / Caesar.
359. Caesar's.
360. The things that are Caesar's.
361. The things that are God's.
362. The Sadducees.
363. If a man dies, leaving a childless wife, his brother must marry the widow. They can then have children who will be considered the dead man's children.
364. Seven.
365. Marry the widow of the eldest brother.
366. Whose wife would the widow be at the resurrection?
367. The scriptures and the power of God.
368. The angels in heaven.
369. Marry.
370. 'I am the God of Abraham, the God of Isaac, and the God of Jacob.'
371. God of the living.
372. A scribe.
373. 'Listen, Israel! The Lord our God is the only Lord. Love the Lord your God with all your heart, with all your soul, with all your mind, and with all your strength.' 'Love your neighbour as yourself.'
374. Animal and other sacrifices.
375. The Kingdom of God.
376. Jesus.
377. Lord.
378. Long robes.
379. The best seats.
380. The worse punishment.
381. In the Temple treasury.
382. Two copper coins, worth a penny.
383. Because she gave all she had to live on.
384. Not one stone will be left in its place.
385. On the Mount of Olives.
386. Many will say 'I am he.' They will claim to speak for Jesus.
387. The gospel must be preached to all peoples / Gentiles.
388. The Holy Spirit.
389. Turn against them and have them put to death.
390. He will be saved.

391. Flee to the hills.
392. Go down to the house to get something.
393. In winter.
394. For the sake of his elect / chosen.
395. False Christs and false prophets.
396. The sun will grow dark; the moon will no longer shine.
397. Clouds.
398. Gather the elect / chosen from one end of the earth to the other.
399. That summer is near.
400. Jesus' words.
401. The Father.
402. Watch / keep awake.
403. Sleeping.
404. The Passover and the Festival of Unleavened Bread.
405. Because the people might riot.
406. Bethany.
407. Simon the leper's house.
408. Pure nard.
409. Because the ointment could have been sold and the money given to the poor.
410. 'You will always have poor people with you, and any time you want to, you can help them.'
411. For burial.
412. Money. (It is not said how much.)
413. A man carrying a water jar in the city.
414. The first day of the Festival of Unleavened Bread. The Passover lambs were killed.
415. The one who would betray him.
416. His body.
417. His blood.
418. The covenant.
419. In the Kingdom of God.
420. To the Mount of Olives.
421. Run away.
422. Peter.
423. Galilee.
424. Peter would deny Jesus three times.
425. Peter, James and John.
426. Abba (GNB: 'My Father').
427. Take the cup away from him.
428. Sleeping.
429. Three.
430. An armed crowd, sent by the Jewish authorities.
431. He would kiss him.
432. A bystander (he is not identified) cut off the ear of the high priest's servant / slave.
433. A young man.
434. To the high priest's courtyard.
435. No.

436. That he would destroy the Temple and build another after three days, that was not built with hands.
437. Nothing.
438. 'I am, and you will all see the Son of Man seated on the right of the Almighty' [Power] 'and coming with the clouds of heaven.'
439. His robe.
440. Blasphemy.
441. He was spat on, blindfolded and beaten. While he was blindfolded, they said, 'Prophesy!' (GNB: 'Guess who hit you!')
442. A servant girl.
443. A cock crowed. (According to most manuscripts of Mark, though some omit this detail.)
444. He was from Galilee.
445. He wept.
446. Pontius.
447. They held a meeting.
448. 'Are you the king of the Jews?'
449. 'So you say.'
450. Nothing.
451. A prisoner who had committed murder during a riot.
452. At Passover.
453. 'Do you want me to release for you the king of the Jews?'
454. Barabbas.
455. Because the chief priests had stirred them up to ask for him.
456. They wanted him crucified.
457. He wanted to please them.
458. He was whipped.
459. They put a purple robe on him and made a crown of thorns. They saluted him, saying, 'Long live the king of the Jews!', beat him, spat on him and bowed to him in homage.
460. The man who carried Jesus' cross.
461. Golgotha. Place of the skull.
462. Wine mixed with myrrh.
463. No.
464. They diced for them.
465. 9 a.m. (the third hour).
466. The King of the Jews.
467. Two robbers.

468. a) 'Aha! You were going to tear down the Temple and build it up again in three days! Now come down from the cross and save yourself!' b) 'He saved others, but he cannot save himself! Let us see the Messiah, the King of Israel, come down from the cross now, and we will believe in him!'
469. Noon (the sixth hour). Three hours.
470. 'Eloi, Eloi, lama sabachthani?' 'My God, my God, why did you abandon me?'
471. Elijah.
472. Vinegar / cheap wine.
473. Because the bystanders wanted to see whether Elijah would come to take him down.
474. The curtain was torn in two, from top to bottom.
475. 'Truly, this man was the Son of God.'
476. The women: Mary Magdalene, Mary the mother of the younger James and of Joseph, and Salome.
477. Joseph of Arimathea.
478. The Kingdom of God.
479. The Sanhedrin.
480. The day of Preparation / the day before the Sabbath.
481. Because Jesus was already dead.
482. Mary Magdalene and Mary the mother of Joseph.
483. To anoint Jesus' body.
484. At sunrise on Sunday morning.
485. Who was going to roll back the stone from the tomb's entrance.
486. A young man, dressed in white.
487. 'He is going to Galilee ahead of you; there you will see him, just as he told you.'
488. Because they were frightened.
489. Mary Magdalene.
490. To two of them.
491. He appeared to the eleven while they were eating and scolded them because they had not believed that he was risen.
492. Preach the gospel to everyone.
493. He was taken up into heaven and sat at God's right hand.

Practice GCSE questions

These are based on the kind of questions set on the exam papers.

You will probably have done many similar questions in class. They can help with your revision, though: when you've revised a topic, it can be very helpful to answer one that's relevant. You can take your time over this and look back at your notes, or answer them with a watch in front of you, allocating them the time you'll have in the exam.

Some questions test what you know and understand. Others ask for your opinion. With the 'opinion' questions, you need to do *exactly* what the question asks, or you'll lose marks. So, if it tells you to explain what someone else might think, and you only say what *you* think, you can't get full marks. It's common for the exam to remind you to back up your views (and those of others) by referring to Mark or to Christianity. You need to do this, too; as the exam is *religious* studies, the examiner will be looking for ideas related to religious principles. Be specific when you refer back to Mark or to Christianity: 'Christians should help the poor because Jesus said people must be nice' is not as good as 'Christians should help the poor because Jesus told the rich man to sell all he had and give to the poor, and because he said they must love their neighbours as themselves'.

The figures in brackets give the number of marks available. These vary between exam boards (it's worth looking up past papers online of the exam board's website). In general, though, one mark answers will require a word or a phrase (don't write more: it won't gain any more marks) and others will need a number of sentences or paragraphs. A 5 mark answer needs to be longer than a 2 mark one!

Remember: not all exam boards set exactly the same areas of study. If the question asks you about something you don't need to know for your exam, leave it out.

For more advice on the exam, see the 'How to revise' section, which begins on page 1.

1. a) Mark says that Jesus was often accompanied by his disciples.
   (i)   Who were Jesus' first two disciples?   (2)
   (ii) What was their job before they were called by Jesus?   (1)
   (iii) Why might Jesus have chosen people like this?   (4)

b) Describe another occasion when Jesus asks someone to become a disciple. (4)

c) On one occasion, Jesus sent out the twelve disciples.
   (i)   State two things he told them to do. (2)
   (ii) What do Jesus' instructions to the disciples here show about the way he expected people to live? (4)

d) 'Jesus asked too much of people. Living up to his expectations is impossible.' Do you agree? Give reasons for your answer, showing that you have thought about more than one point of view. You must refer to Mark's Gospel or Christianity in your answer. (5)

2. a) Jesus asked Levi to follow him.
   (i)   What was Levi's occupation? (1)
   (ii) Why were people shocked when Jesus ate with Levi? (3)
   (iii) What did Jesus say to them? (3)

b) How might this story help Christians today to understand about the need for community cohesion / good relationships with different groups in society? (4)

c) 'Jesus never condemned anyone.' Do you agree? Explain your answer. (3)

3. Mark begins his Gospel with an account of John the Baptist's teaching.
a) What was John preparing people for and how did he do this? (3)
b) What did John say about himself and about the one who was to come after him? (3)
c) What happened when Jesus was baptised? (4)
d) How can the story of Jesus' baptism help to explain the idea of the Trinity? (4)

e) 'The story of Jesus' baptism is too far fetched. I just don't believe it.' What do you think? Give reasons for your answer, showing that you have considered more than one viewpoint. You must refer to Mark's Gospel in your answer. (5)

4. a) When Jesus preached in his home town, people rejected him.
    (i) What were they saying about him? (3)
    (ii) What did Jesus say to them? (2)

   b) At Caesarea Philippi, Peter said that Jesus was the Messiah or Christ. Explain what this title means. (5)

   c) 'Get behind me, Satan!' Why did Jesus say this to Peter? (2)

   d) ' "The Messiah" is the most important title for Jesus and it says all there is to say.' Do you agree? Give reasons for your answer and show that you have thought about another viewpoint. Refer to Mark's Gospel in your answer. (5)

5. Mark says Jesus took Peter, James and John with him up a high mountain.
   a) Outline what happened on the mountain. (6)
   b) What does this story show about who Jesus was? (4)
   c) The disciples were frightened by what they saw. Retell another story from Mark's Gospel when people were frightened. (5)
   d) 'Christians should never be frightened.' Do you agree? Give reasons for your answer and show that you have thought about another viewpoint. Refer to Mark's Gospel in your answer. (5)

6. Mark tells how on one occasion Jesus calmed a storm.
   a) Retell the incident. (5)
   b) How could this story help Christians who are being attacked for their faith today? (4)
   c) On another occasion, Jesus cured a man who was possessed by a Legion (Good News Bible: 'Mob') of demons. Outline the story. (8)
   d) 'No-one can believe in possession by demons today.' Do you agree? Explain your reasons and show why someone might disagree with you. Refer to Mark's Gospel in your answer. (5)

7. a) Outline what happened when Jesus healed a leper. (5)
   b) Retell **one** occasion in Mark when Jesus healed a blind man. (4)

c) Retell what happened when Jesus healed Simon Peter's mother-in-law. (3)

d) Why is it important that Jesus healed people like these? (4)

e) 'Jesus' miracles were all made up.' Do you agree? Give reasons for your answer, showing that you have considered more than one point of view. Refer to Mark's Gospel in your answer. (5)

8. a) Mark often describes the arguments between Jesus and the Pharisees. Describe one such argument. (5)

b) What was the difference between the Pharisees' and Jesus' attitude to the Jewish Law? (5)

c) Mark says Jesus only had one argument with the Sadducees. Outline what happened. (6)

d) 'Jesus' arguments with the Jewish authorities show that you can't trust people in power.' Do you agree? Give reasons for your answer, showing that you have thought about more than one point of view. Refer to Christianity / Mark's Gospel in your answer. (5)

9. a) Outline what Jesus taught about marriage and divorce. (4)

b) How was this different from what Jewish people believed at the time? (3)

c) 'Jesus' teaching about marriage is too hard to keep.' Do you agree? Explain your reasons. (3)

10. a) 'What comes out of a person is what makes a person unclean.' What did Jesus mean by this? (3)

b) Jesus' attitude to sinners was different from that of people of his time. Retell one story which shows this. (5)

c) Mark describes how Jesus spoke against the religious leaders in the parable of the vineyard. Outline this parable. (5)

d) 'Jesus was too harsh about the religious leaders of his time.' Do you agree? Give reasons for your answer, showing that you have thought about more than one point of view. Refer to Mark's Gospel in your answer. (5)

11. a) Retell the parable of the sower. (5)

b) How does Mark say Jesus explained this parable? (5)

c) Outline the parable of the seed growing secretly. (3)

d) Explain one idea about the Kingdom of God contained within the parable of the seed growing secretly. (3)

e) 'It wasn't fair for Jesus to talk in parables. He should have just said what he meant.' Do you think this is correct? Explain your answer. (3)

12. a) Mark describes how Jesus told a rich man to sell all he had, give the money to the poor, and follow him.

(i) What did the rich man then do? (2)

(ii) What did Jesus say to the disciples when this happened? (2)

(iii) How did the disciples react to Jesus' words? (2)

b) On another occasion, Jesus saw a widow in the Temple. Retell this story. (4)

c) 'Lots of people call themselves Christians but they don't follow what Jesus taught about wealth and money.' Do you agree? Give reasons for your answer, showing that you have thought about more than one point of view. Refer to Mark's Gospel in your answer. (5)

13. Mark says Jesus' disciples argued about which one of them was the greatest.

a) Retell this incident. (4)

b) Why might Jesus have thought that a child was the best model for his disciples? (2)

c) James and John asked Jesus to grant them a request. Outline this story. (5)

d) 'The greatest people in the world are those who have the most power.' Do you agree? Give reasons for your answer, showing that you have thought about more than one point of view. You must refer to Mark's Gospel / Christianity in your answer. (5)

14. a) Retell what happened when Jesus ate the Last Supper with his disciples. (5)

b) Describe how Christians today re-enact the Last Supper when they worship. (8)

   c) 'Going to the Eucharist (or the Mass) doesn't matter. Living a Christian life is much more important.' Do you agree? Give reasons for your answer, showing that you have thought about more than one point of view. You must refer to Mark's Gospel in your answer. (5)

15. a) What happens at a service of infant baptism? (3)
   b) What happens at a believer's (adult) baptism? (4)
   c) Why do Christians think it is important to be baptised? (5)
   d) 'Christians should not baptise babies. They should wait until people are grown up.' Do you agree? Give reasons for your answer, showing that you have thought about more than one point of view. (5)

16. a) Outline:
     i) Jesus' trial before the Sanhedrin (5)
     ii) Jesus' trial before Pilate, including the conversation Pilate had with the crowd. (5)
   b) 'Eloi, Eloi, lama sabachthani?' What does this mean? (2)
   c) When Jesus died, what did the Roman centurion (army officer) say? (2)
   d) Why is Jesus' death important for Christians? (7)
   d) 'Pilate was a coward. He should have released Jesus.' Do you agree? Explain your answer. (3)

17. a) Early in the morning, after the Sabbath, Mark says the women went to Jesus' tomb. Describe what happened, up to the point when the women run away. (6)
   b) The final chapter of Mark describes the appearances of the risen Jesus. State two people or groups of people who Jesus appeared to. (2)
   c) Why is the resurrection important to Christians? (6)
   d) 'The resurrection of Jesus cannot have happened.' Do you agree? Give reasons for your answer, showing that you have thought about more than one point of view. Refer to Mark's Gospel in your answer. (5)

The Today Series:
GCSE RS textbooks from St Mark's Press

£14.75 each; £10 each for 5 copies or more

Inspection copies available: please email info@stmarkspress.com

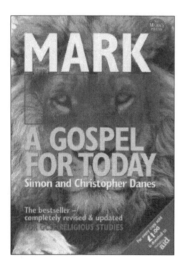

The Lion edition of
Mark: A Gospel for Today

Mark: A Gospel for Today
Simon and Christopher Danes
Third edition
ISBN 978-1-907062-00-1, A4, 194 pages

The bestseller, formerly from Lion Publishing, now from St Mark's Press. Totally revised and updated and designed for *all* exam specifications which set Mark's Gospel for GCSE.

'Brings the pages of Mark to life. Many generations of students have been inspired by *Mark: A Gospel for Today* – a *must have* textbook for anyone taking GCSE Religious Studies'
Gill Smith, Head of RE, King's School, Ely

'The readers are constantly stimulated; their attention is constantly re-engaged. Yet this is achieved without sacrificing scholarship or intellectual rigour. Information is clearly presented... content is made accessible to the less able, yet there is plenty to challenge those who can go further... Questions are carefully prepared, and the readers cannot escape the challenge to think for themselves... Catering for a wide ability range and engaging the interest of all.'
Review of the first edition from *British Journal of Religious Education*

Today's Issues and Christian Beliefs
Simon and Christopher Danes
ISBN 978-1-907062-02-5, A4, 190 pages

The highly commended and popular textbook, previously published by Lion, with over 100,000 copies sold.

Totally revised and updated and **suitable for *all* exam boards.** To meet the needs of the current GCSE specifications, 75% of the material in this new edition is entirely new!

Suitable for moral issues papers from the standpoints of both Christianity as a whole and Roman Catholicism.

Includes first person accounts from people who were actively involved in the areas studied.

'Packed full of information... A significant amount of the material is simply not found in other school textbooks. The personal accounts and stories are also particularly helpful for engaging and informing students. I'm much enjoying using it.'

> Andrew Dalton, Head of RE,
> Shrewsbury School

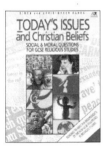

The Lion edition of
Today's Issues and Christian Beliefs

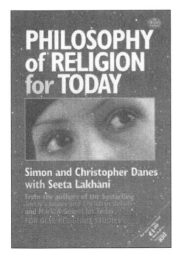

Philosophy of Religion for Today
Simon and Christopher Danes
with Seeta Lakhani
ISBN 978-1-907062-05-6, A4, 160 pages

This is a GCSE textbook which also provides an accessible introduction for A Level students.

'*Philosophy of Religion for Today* is a welcome addition to the range of books now on offer for GCSE Religious Studies. The images and drawings are refreshing and the text is a particular strength. The conversational style is absorbing, while difficult concepts are clearly and painstakingly explained, using imaginative examples pupils can understand. It is both accessible and scholarly.'

Elizabeth McCaul, Head of RE, The Princess Helena College, Hitchin

For further study:

Books by William Barclay

William Barclay is one of the most popular of Christian writers and scholars, second only, perhaps, to C. S. Lewis. His books have sold over 17 million copies. St Mark's Press currently publishes three of his best titles and we are in negotiation with the Barclay estate to publish many more. They are suitable for teachers, A Level students, and for all those who want to find out more about the Bible.

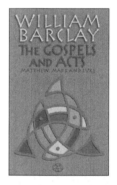

The Gospels and Acts:
Matthew, Mark and Luke
ISBN 978-1-907062-06-3
RRP £14.95   Paperback

The Gospels and Acts:
John and Acts
ISBN 978-1-907062-07-0
RRP £14.95   Paperback

Masterly: two of the best books on the New Testament ever written.

Professor Barclay's study takes the reader effortlessly, gently and wisely through the theories, speculation, guesswork – and findings – of New Testament studies. It is an absorbing guide which will be enjoyed by anyone with an interest in the Bible.

The Mind of St Paul
ISBN 978-1-907062-08-7
RRP £11.95   Paperback

Paul's letters are the earliest Christian documents and his contribution to the development of Christianity cannot be overstated. Professor Barclay's guide explains clearly how Paul attempted to deal with the turbulent issues of his own day and how Paul's convictions about the work of Christ informed his response. A genuinely readable introduction to a major thinker of the first century.